Fun and Easy! Korean Vocabulary Quiz Workbook

For permission requests, write us at

marketing@newampersand.com

Ordering Information: Quantity sales.
Special discounts are available on quantity purchases by corporations, associations, and others.
For details, contact the publisher at the email address above.

Printed in the United States of America

ISBN-13: 979-11-88195-48-0

TABLE OF CONTENTS

WORD & PICTURE MATCHING QUESTIONS

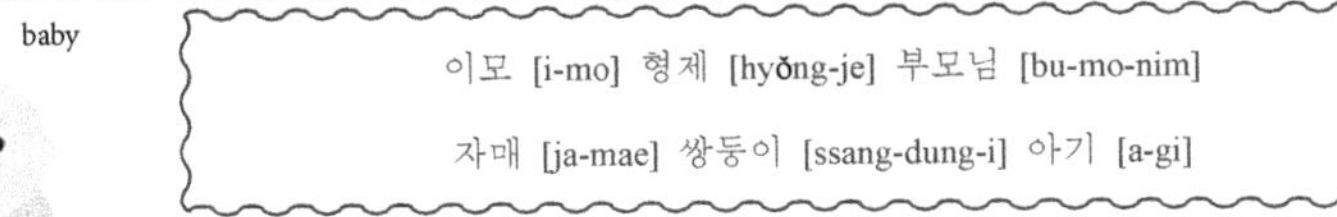

baby

aunt

twins

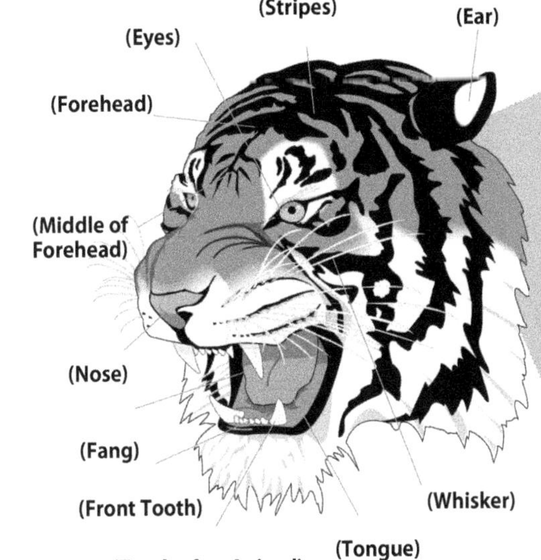

Word & Picture matching questions are a fun and intuitive way to expand your vocabulary. Choose a word from the box and match the correct picture!

FILL IN THE BLANKS QUESTIONS

Fill in the blanks is a great way to build your vocabulary and learn Korean sentences at the same time!

4. (   )을 씻었다.
[(   )-ŭl ssi-sŏt-da.]
I washed my (face).

1. 코 [ko] 2. 머리 [mŏ-ri] 3. 얼굴 [ŏl-gul] 4. 귀 [gwi] 5. 다리 [da-ri]

KOREAN VOCAB WORKBOOK
MATCHING HOMONYMS

Some Korean words sound the same but have different meanings! Learn these essential homonyms and double up your vocabulary arsenal!

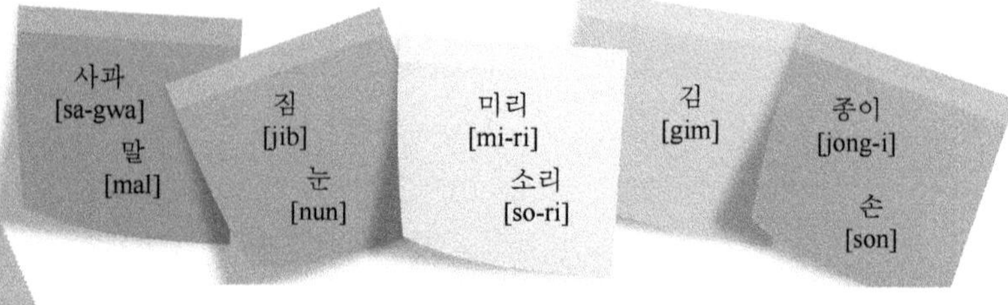

horse

language/word

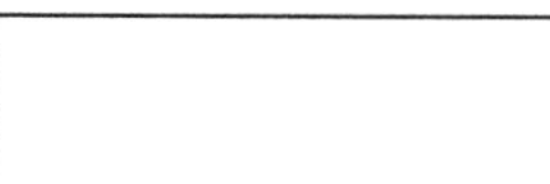

KOREAN VOCAB WORKBOOK
MATCHING SYNONYMS

기쁨 [gi-bbŭm]	○	○	분노 [bun-no]
화 [hwa]	○	○	감정 [gam-jŏng]
느낌 [nŭ-kkim]	○	○	인간 [in-gan]

There are more than one way to say something! Matching synonyms are an efficient way to learn them all!

KOREAN VOCAB WORKBOOK
MATCHING ANTONYMS

Every word has its counterpart! Learn the antonyms to stimulate your brain and broaden your vocabulary!

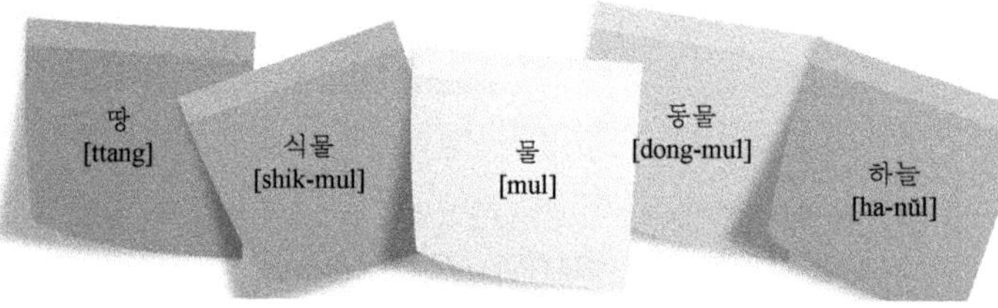

( )
animal

( )
plant

CROSSWORD PUZZLES

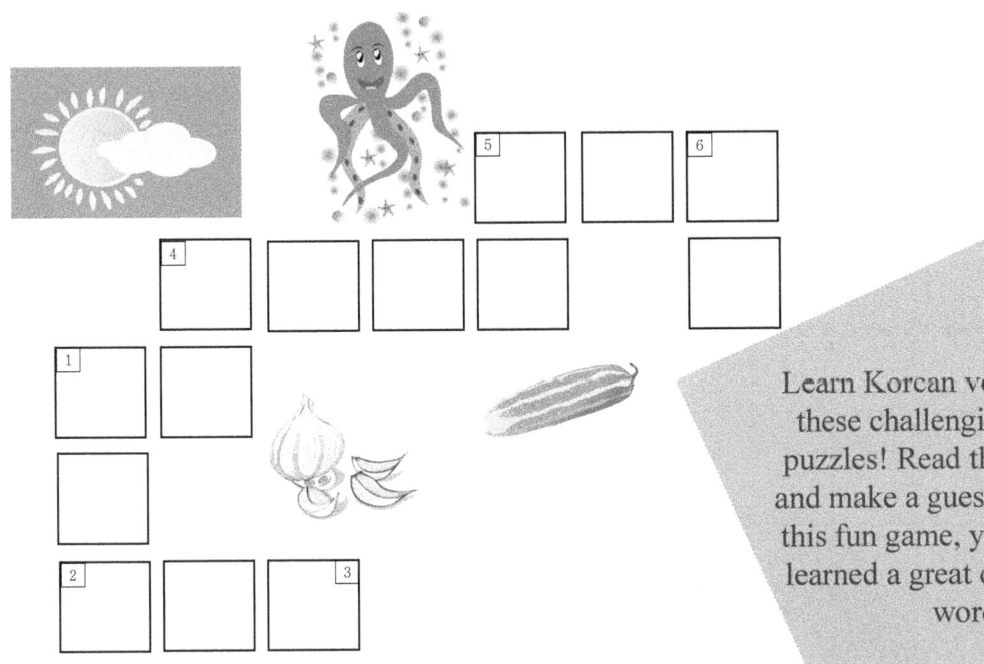

Learn Korean vocabulary with these challenging crossword puzzles! Read the descriptions and make a guess. At the end of this fun game, you would have learned a great deal of Korean words!

KOREAN VOCAB WORKBOOK

MULTIPLE QUESTIONS

Try these good ol' multiple questions to test your Korean vocabulary! Some of the questions are quite tricky! But through challenges you learn most!

No.	Word	Option	Option
1	dentist's office	사과 [sa-gwa]	치과 [chi-gwa]
		백화점 [baek-hwa-jŏm]	학원 [hak-won]
2	eraser	연필 [yŏn-pil]	공책 [gong-chaek]
		지우개 [ji-u-gae]	분필 [bun-pil]
3	green tea	홍차 [hong-cha]	모과차 [mo-gwa-cha]
		맥주 [maek-ju]	녹차 [nok-cha]
4	audience	관중 [gwan-jung]	이모 [i-mo]
		학생 [hak-saeng]	사장님 [sa-jang-nim]

이모 [i-mo] 형제 [hyŏng-je] 부모님 [bu-mo-nim]

자매 [ja-mae] 쌍둥이 [ssang-dung-i] 아기 [a-gi]

삼촌 [sam-chon] 아빠 [a-bba]

할아버지 [hal-a-bŏ-ji] 엄마 [ŏm-ma] 할머니 [hal-mŏ-ni]

목수 [mok-su] 경찰관 [gyŏng-chal-gwan] 음악가 [ŭm-ak-ga]

우체부 [u-che-bu] 소방관 [so-bang-gwan] 가수 [ga-su]

과학자 [gwa-hak-ja] 기술자 [gi-sul-ja] 의사 [ŭi-sa]

이발사 [i-bal-sa] 요리사 [yo-ri-sa] 미용사 [mi-yong-sa]

engineer

scientist

doctor

cook/chef

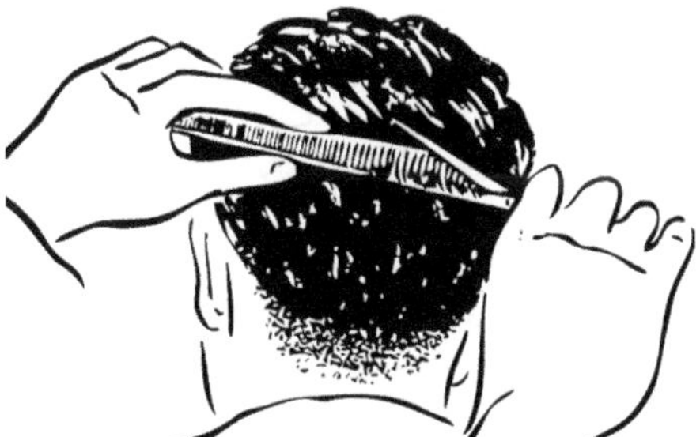

hair dresser

barber

사진사 [sa-jin-sa] 어부 [ŏ-bu] 학생 [hak-saeng]

연기자 [yŏn-gi-ja] 선생님 [sŏn-saeng-nim] 간호사 [gan-ho-sa]

재단사 [jae-dan-sa] 배관공 [bae-gwan-gong] 주부 [ju-bu]

운동선수 [un-dong-sŏn-su] 농부 [nong-bu] 경비원 [gyŏng-bi-won]

신부님 [shin-bu-nim] 환자 [hwan-ja] 사서 [sa-sŏ]

은행원 [ŭn-haeng-wŏn] 수녀님 [su-nyŏ-nim]

librarian

catholic father

patient

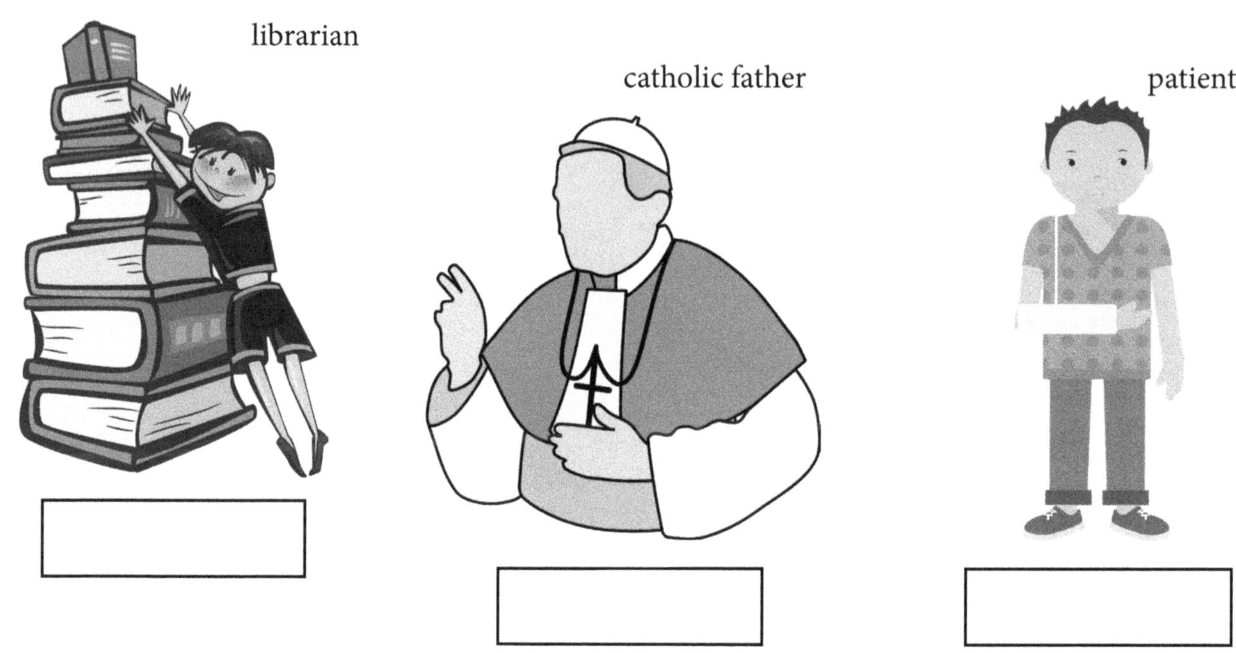

nun

banker

눈 [nun] 줄무늬 [jul-mu-nŭi] 귀 [gwi] 이마 [i-ma] 미간 [mi-gan]

코 [ko] 송곳니 [song-got-ni] 앞니 [ap-ni] 이빨 [i-bbal] 혀 [hyŏ] 수염 [su-yŏm]

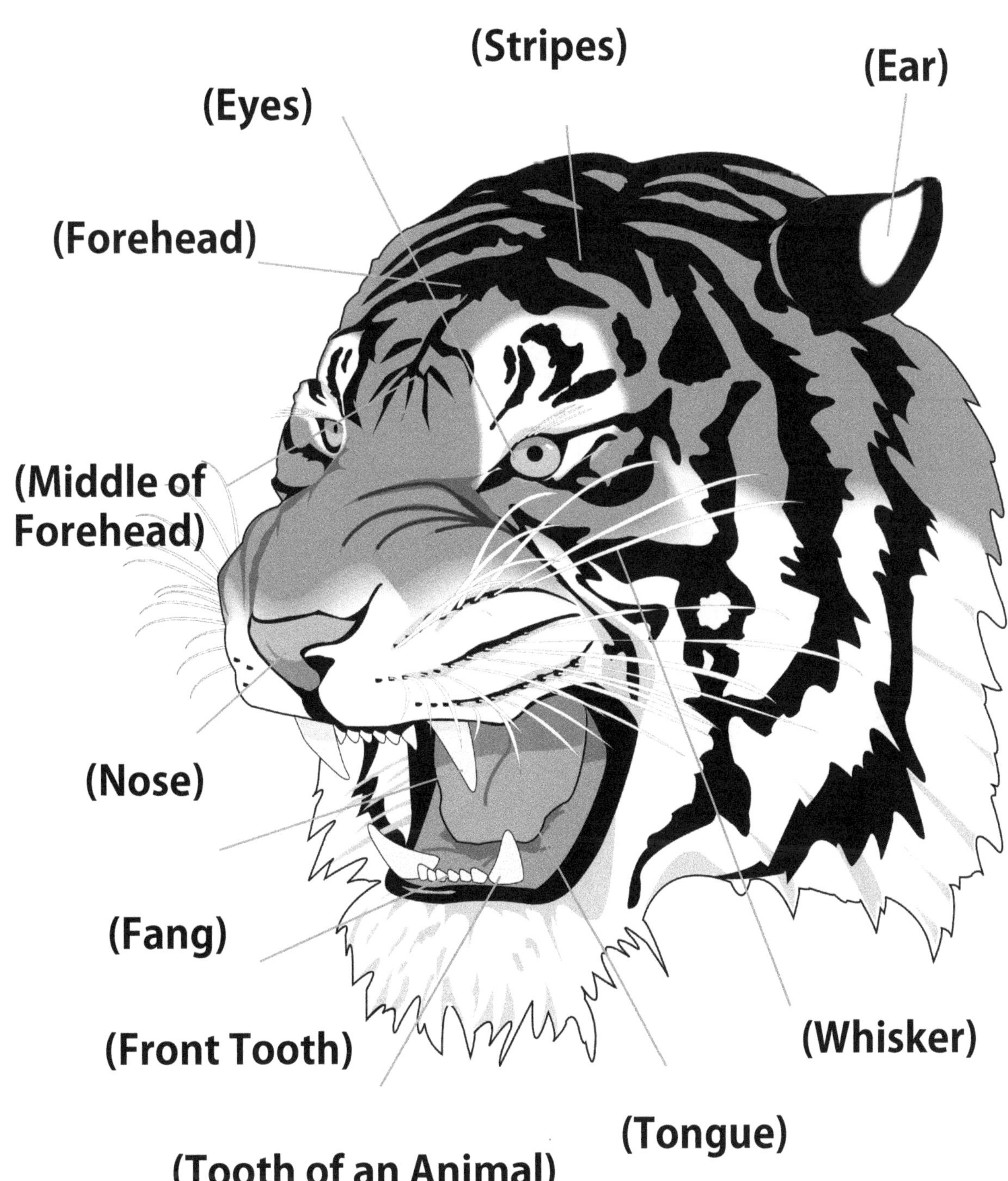

나무늘보 [na-mu-nŭl-bo] 코끼리 [ko-kki-ri] 기린 [gi-rin]

코뿔소 [ko-bbul-so] 사자 [sa-ja] 소 [so]

말 [mal] 양 [yang] 개 [gae]

토끼 [to-kki] 고양이 [go-yang-i] 원숭이 [wŏn-sung-i]

눈 [nun] 이마 [i-ma] 귓볼 [gwit-bol] 턱 [tok] 보조개 [bo-jo-gae]
콧구멍 [kot-gu-mŏng] 인중 [in-jung] 홍채 [hong-chae] 광대뼈 [gwang-dae-bbyŏ]
턱선 [tŏk-sŏn] 입술 [ip-sul] 머리카락 [mŏ-ri-ka-rak] 가르마 [ga-rŭ-ma]
구레나룻 [gu-re-na-rut] 이 [i] 귀 [gwi] 코 [ko] 눈썹 [nun-ssŏp]

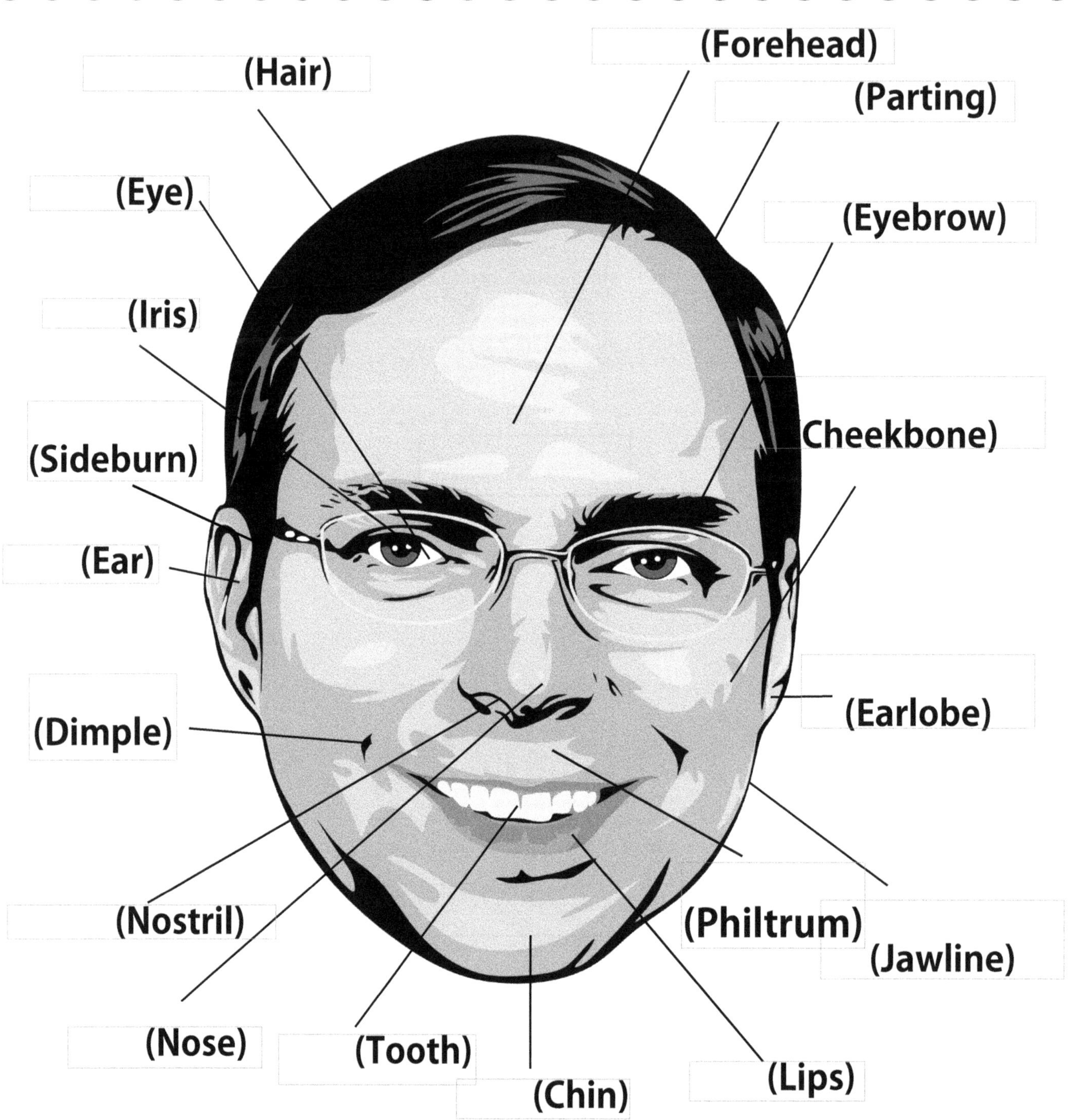

목 [mok] 가슴 [ga-sŭm] 손 [son] 무릎 [mu-rŭp]
팔꿈치 [pal-kkum-chi] 다리 [da-ri] 얼굴 [ŏl-gul] 허리 [ho-ri] 팔 [pal]
허벅지 [hŏ-bŏk-ji] 골반 [gol-ban] 정강이 [jŏng-gang-i]
복부 [bok-bu] 발 [bal] 머리 [mŏ-ri] 어깨 [ŏ-kkae]

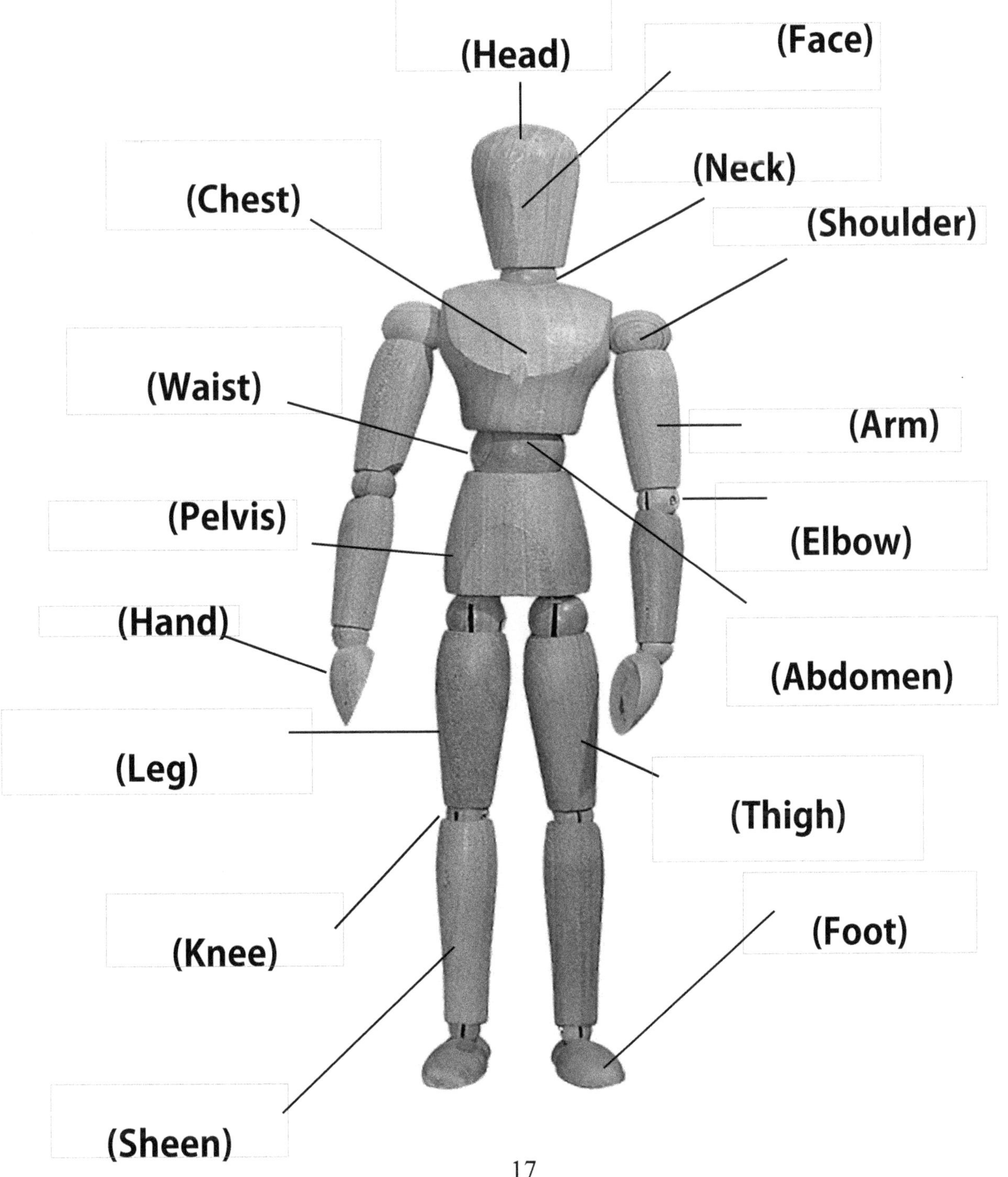

약 손가락 [yak son-ga-rak] 엄지 [ŏm-ji] 손톱 [son-top]
손날 [son-nal] 가운뎃 손가락 [ga-un-det son-ga-rak] 팔목 [pal-mok]
집게 손가락 [jip-ge son-ga-rak] 손바닥 [son-ba-dak]
새끼 손가락 [sae-kki son-ga-rak]

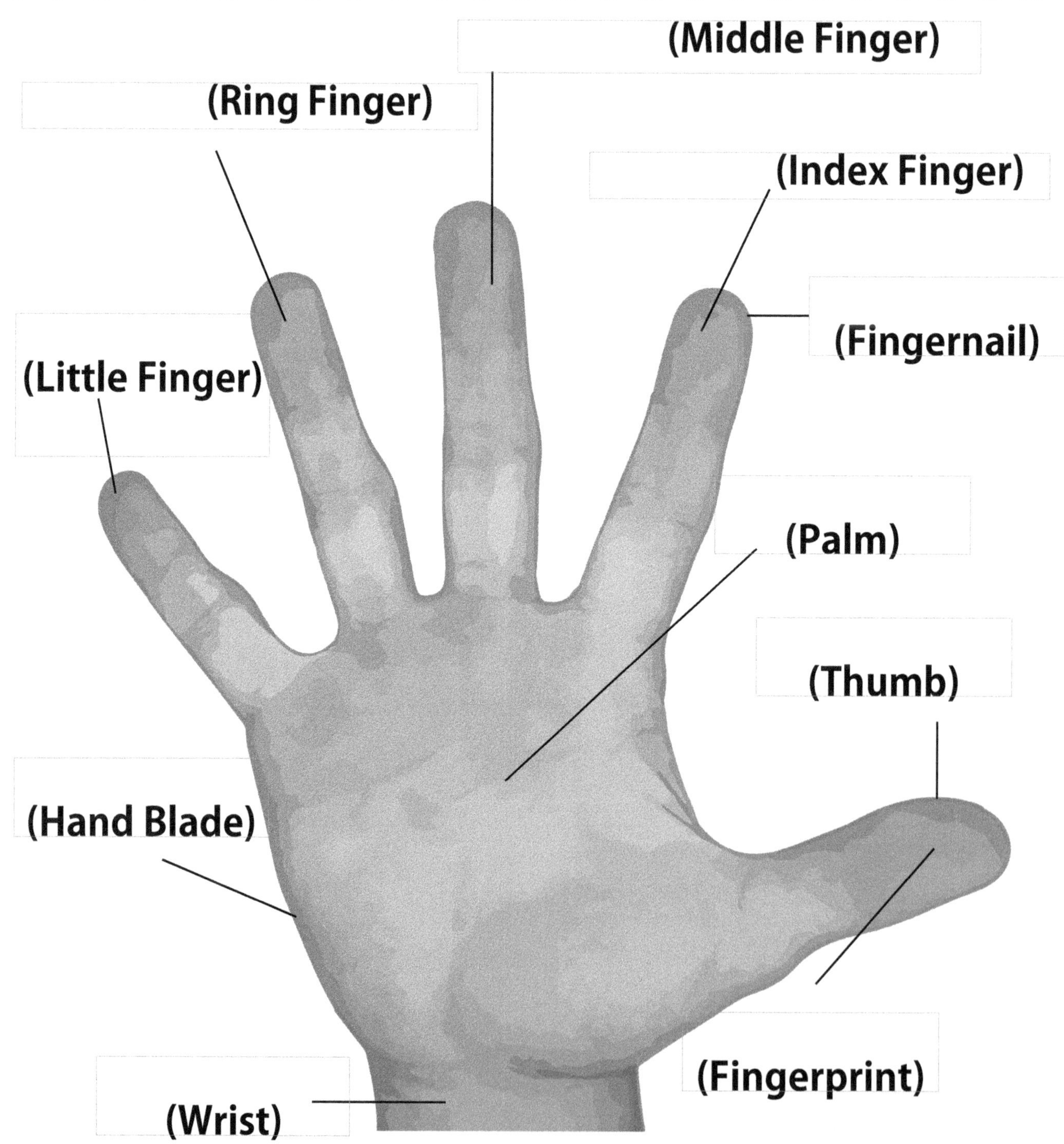

발톱 [bal-top] 새끼 발가락 [sae-kki bal-ga-rak] 둘째 발가락 [dul-jjae bal-ga-rak]
가운뎃 발가락 [ga-un-det bal-ga-rak] 엄지 발가락 [ŏm-ji bal-ga-rak]
발바닥 [bal-ba-dak] 넷째 발가락 [net-jjae bal-ga-rak]
발등 [bal-dŭng] 발뒤꿈치 [bal dwi-kkum-chi]

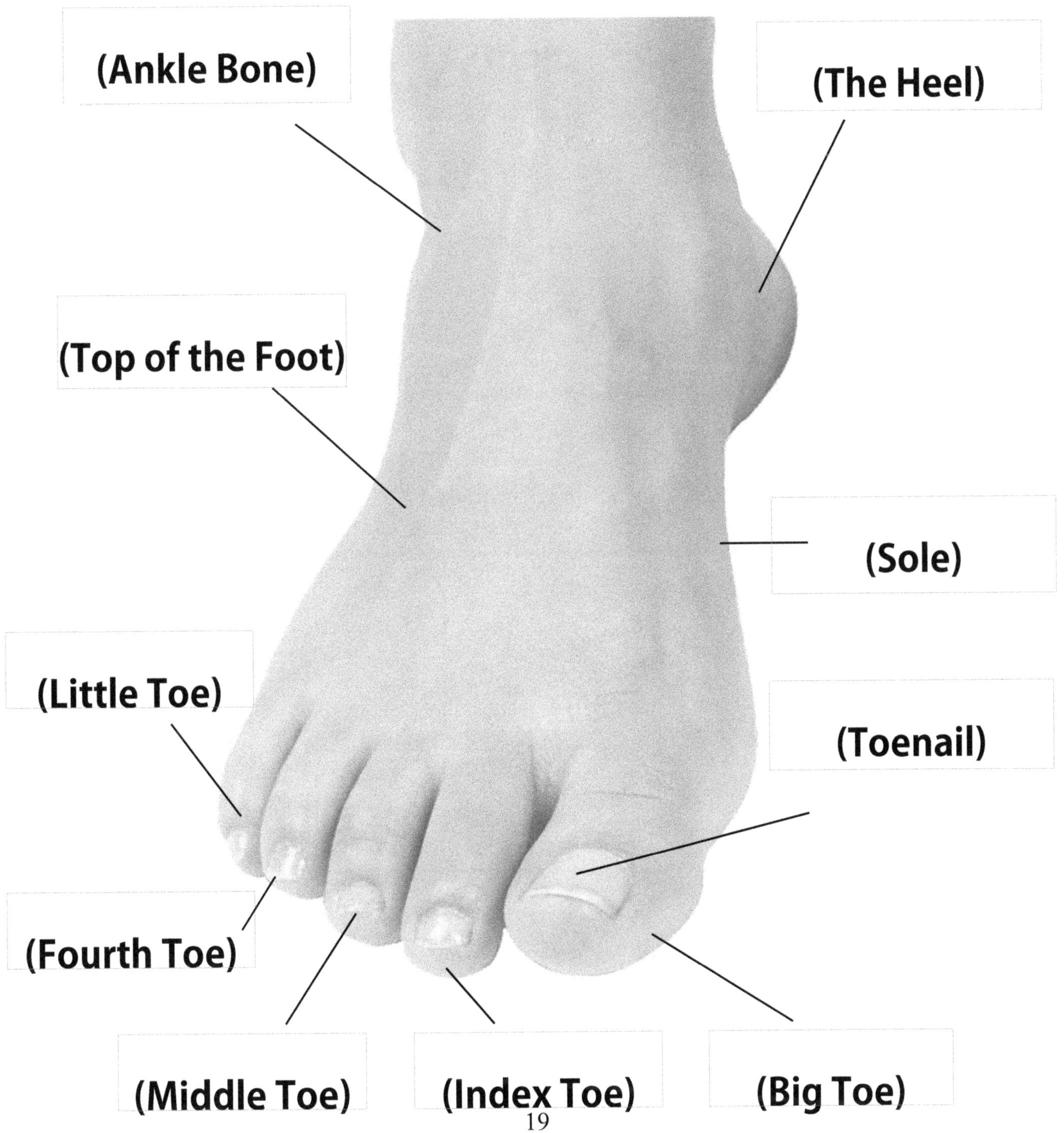

차고 [cha-go] 거실 [gŏ-sil] 침실 [chim-sil]

욕실 [yok-sil] 부엌 [bu-ŏk] 지붕 [ji-bung]

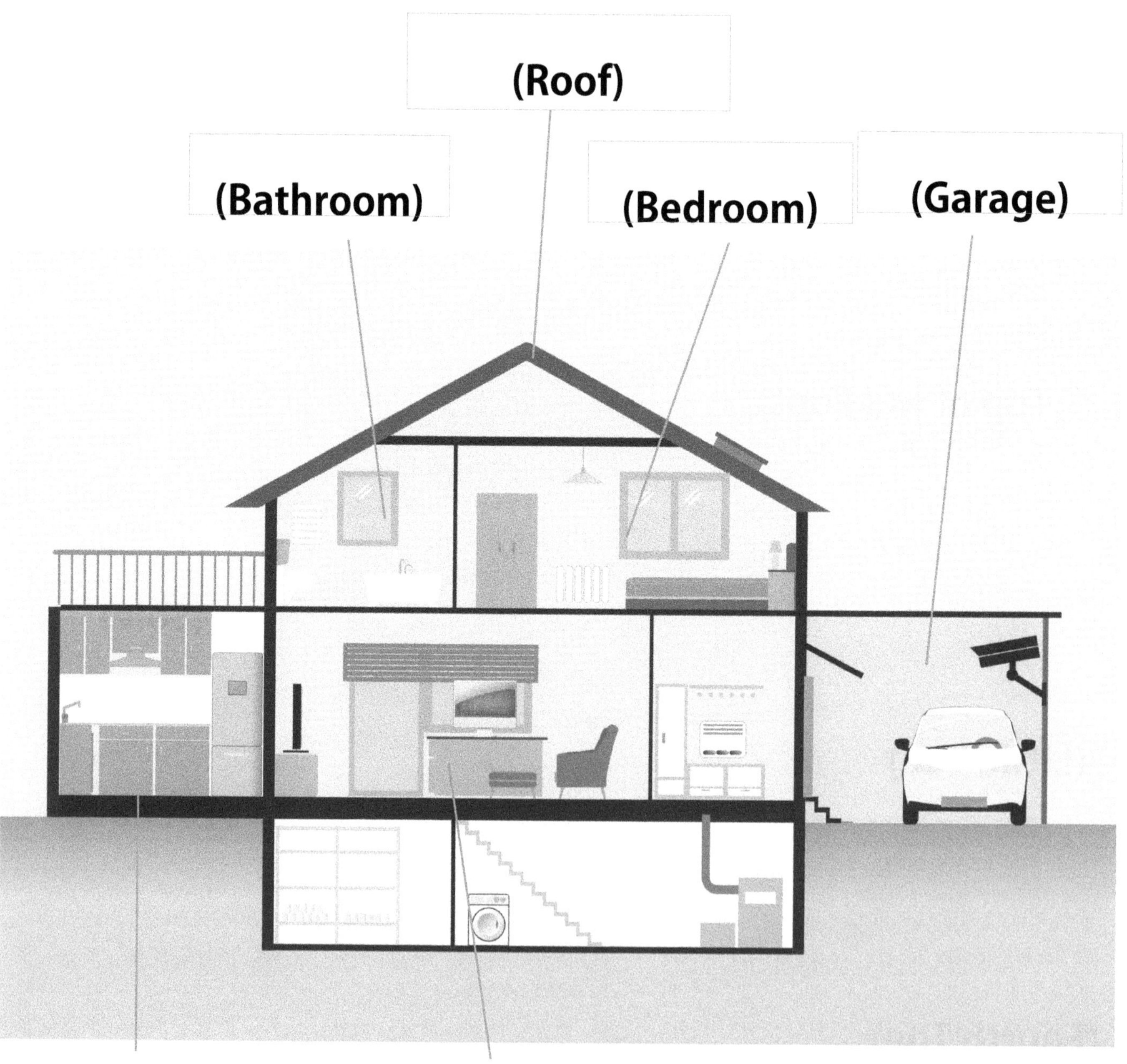

오토바이 [o-to-ba-i] 지하철 [ji-ha-chŏl] 기차 [gi-cha]

비행기 [bi-haeng-gi] 자전거 [ja-jŏn-gŏ] 버스 [bŏ-sŭ]

(Airplane)

(Bus)

(Bicycle)

(Motorcycle)

(Train)

(Subway)

공휴일 [gong-hyu-il] 주말 [ju-mal] 달/월 [dal/wŏl] 날짜 [nal-jja]

주중/평일 [ju-jung/pyŏng-il] 년/연도 [nyŏn/yŏn-do]

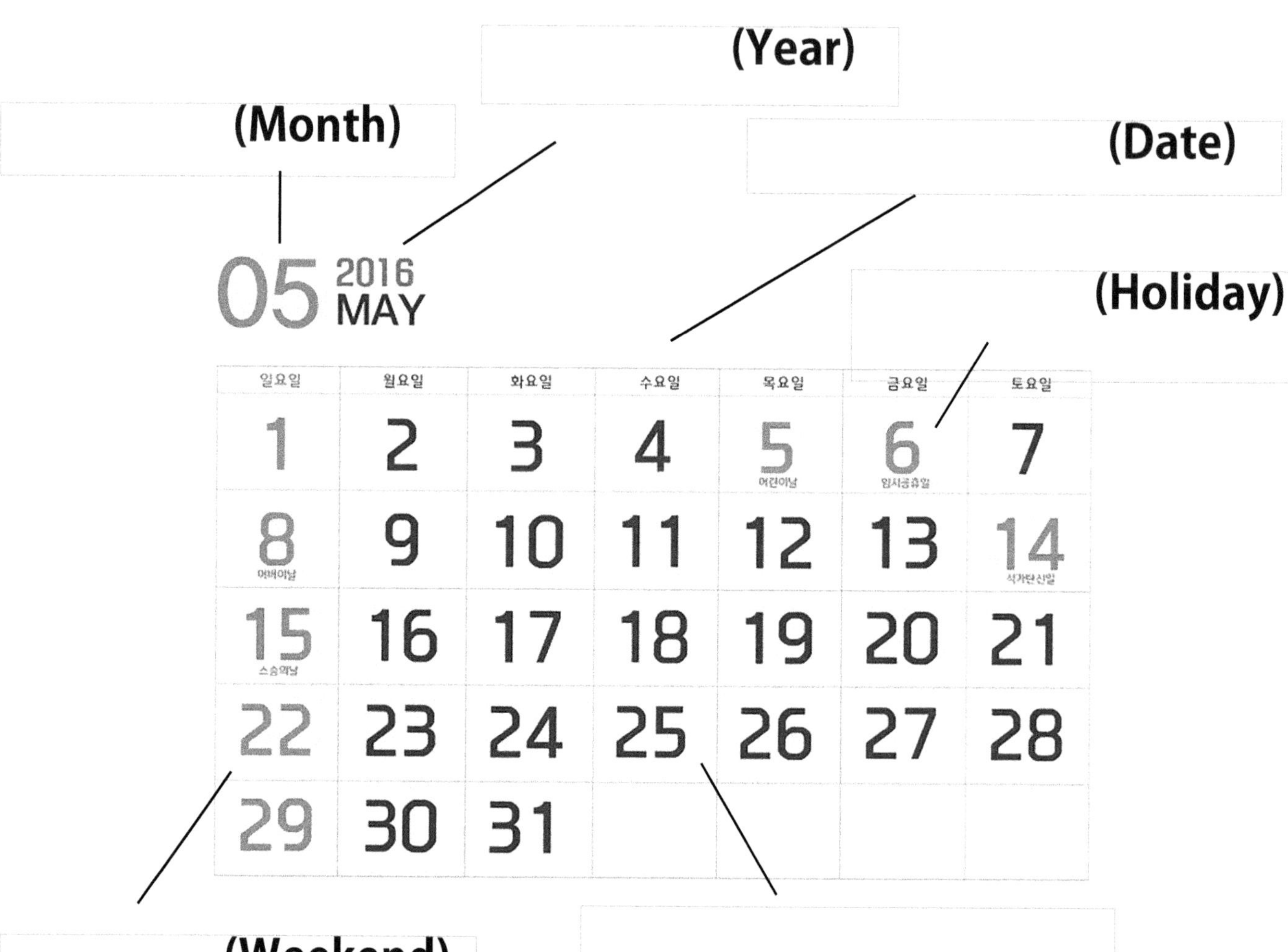

화요일 [hwa-yo-il] 월요일 [wŏl-yo-il] 토요일 [to-yo-il]

수요일 [su-yo-il] 일요일 [il-yo-il] 목요일 [mok-yo-il] 금요일 [gŭm-yo-il]

(Monday) (Tuesday) (Wednesday)

(Thursday) (Friday) (Saturday) (Sunday)

종업원 [jong-ŏp-won] 손님 [son-nim] 식탁 [shik-tak]

찻잔 [chat-jan] 미간 [mi-gan] 주문서 [ju-mun-sŏ]

칫솔 [chit-sol] 수건 [su-gŏn] 샤워실 [sha-wŏ-sil] 면도기 [myŏn-do-gi]

휴지 [hyu-ji] 목욕 가운 [mok-yok ga-un] 욕조 [yok-jo]

체중계 [che-jung-gye] 비누 [bi-nu] 세면대 [se-myŏn-dae]

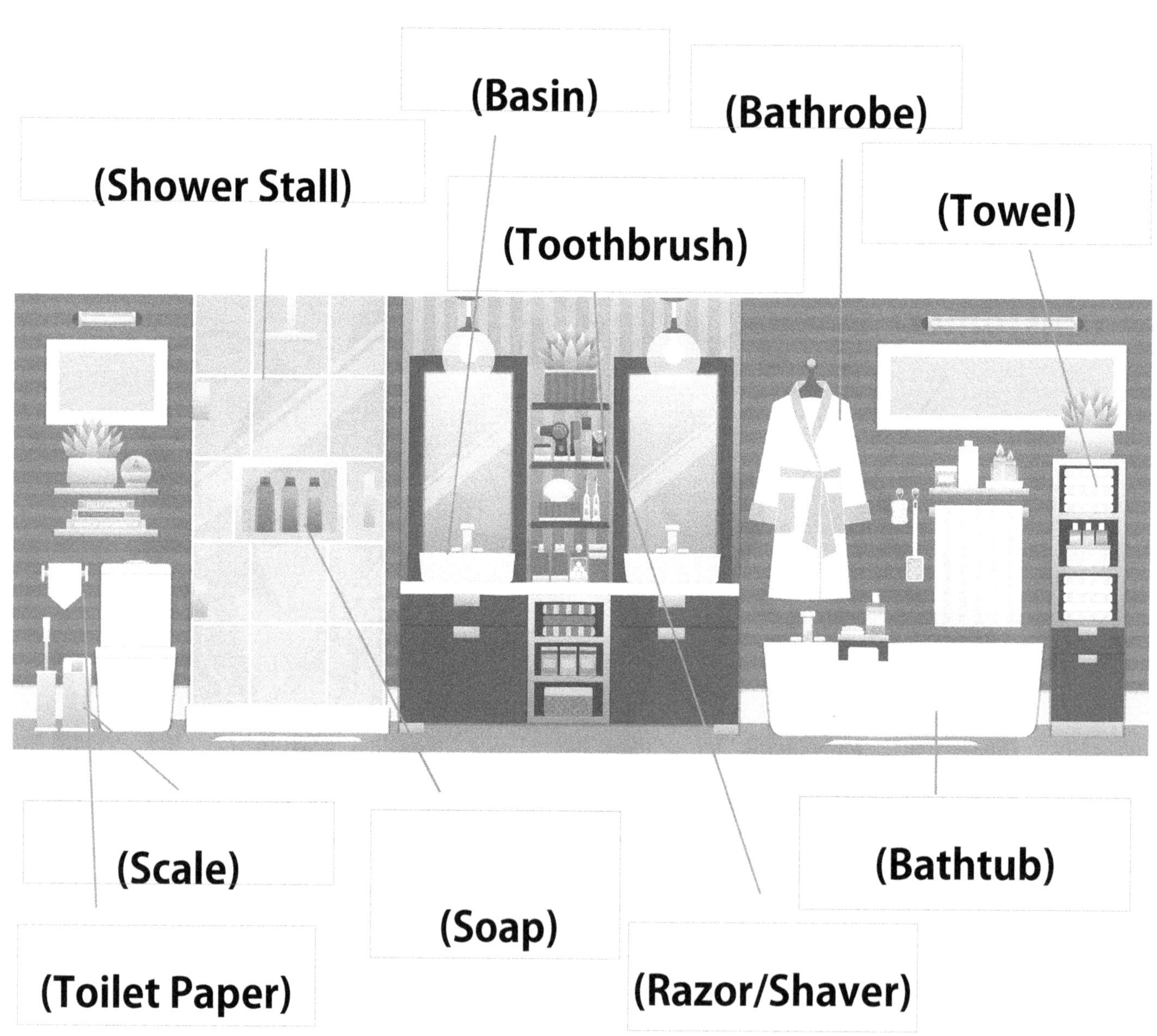

ANSWER KEY

baby
아기 [a-gi]
aunt
이모 [i-mo]
twins
쌍둥이 [ssang-dung-i]
mother
엄마 [ǒm-ma]
father
아빠 [a-bba]
parents
부모님 [bu-mo-nim]
brothers
형제 [hyǒng-je]
sisters
자매 [ja-mae]
grandmother
할머니 [hal-mǒ-ni]
grandfather
할아버지 [hal-a-bǒ-ji]
uncle
삼촌 [sam-chon]
fire figther
소방관 [so-bang-gwan]
police officer
경찰관 [gyǒng-chal-gwan]
mailman
우체부 [u-che-bu]
engineer
기술자 [gi-sul-ja]
scientist
과학자 [gwa-hak-ja]
doctor
의사 [ŭi-sa]
musician
음악가 [ŭm-ak-ga]
singer
가수 [ga-su]
carpenter
목수 [mok-su]
barber
이발사 [i-bal-sa]
hair dresser
미용사 [mi-yong-sa]
cook/chef
요리사 [yo-ri-sa]

teacher
선생님 [sŏn-saeng-nim]
student
학생 [hak-saeng]
fisherman
어부 [ŏ-bu]
photographer
사진사 [sa-jin-sa]
nurse
간호사 [gan-ho-sa]
actor
연기자 [yŏn-gi-ja]

tailor
재단사 [jae-dan-sa]
athlete
운동선수 [un-dong-sŏn-su]
plumber
배관공 [bae-gwan-gong]
housewife
주부 [ju-bu]
farmer
농부 [nong-bu]
security officer
경비원 [gyŏng-bi-won]

librarian
사서 [sa-sŏ]
catholic father
신부님 [shin-bu-nim]
patient
환자 [hwan-ja]
nun
수녀님 [su-nyŏ-nim]
banker
은행원 [ŭn-haeng-wŏn]

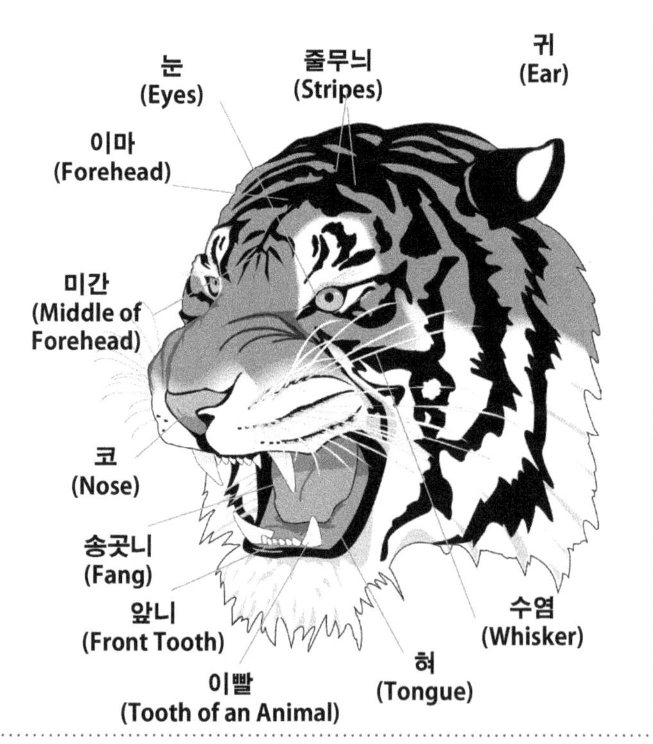
눈
(Eyes)
줄무늬
(Stripes)
귀
(Ear)
이마
(Forehead)
미간
(Middle of Forehead)
코
(Nose)
송곳니
(Fang)
앞니
(Front Tooth)
이빨
(Tooth of an Animal)
혀
(Tongue)
수염
(Whisker)

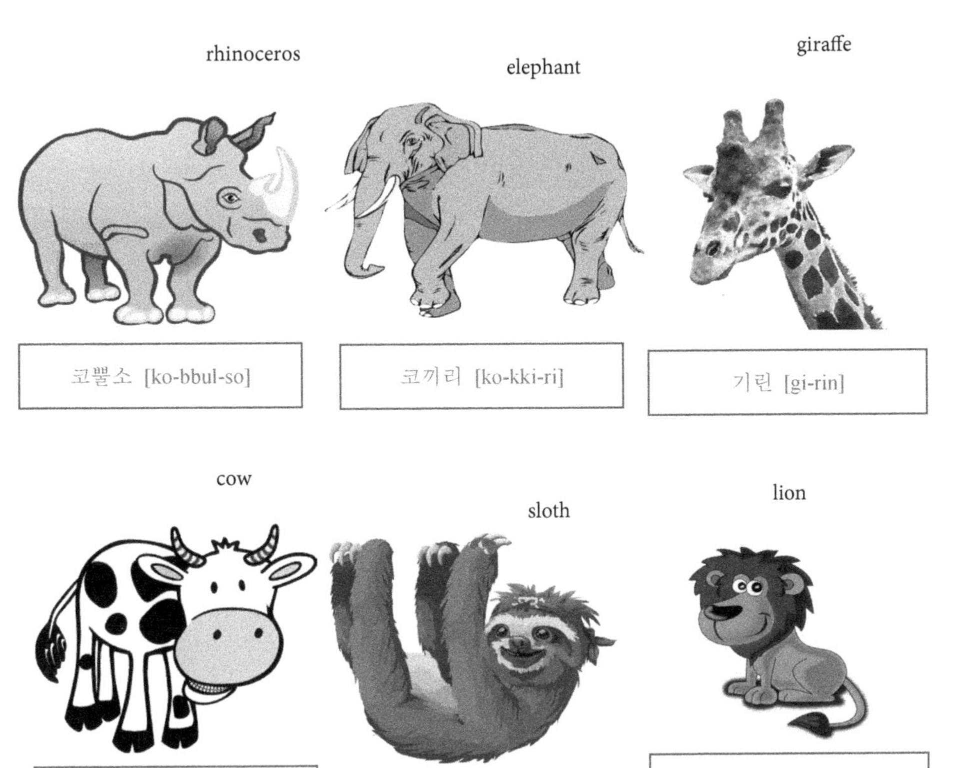

rhinoceros

코뿔소 [ko-bbul-so]

elephant

코끼리 [ko-kki-ri]

giraffe

기린 [gi-rin]

cow

소 [so]

sloth

나무늘보 [na-mu-nŭl-bo]

lion

사자 [sa-ja]

sheep

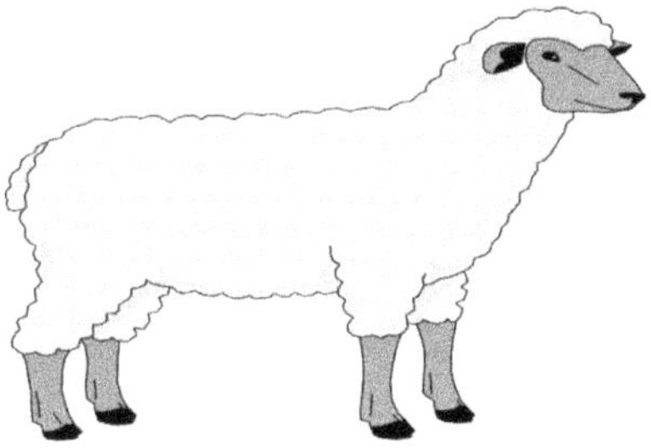

양 [yang]

horse

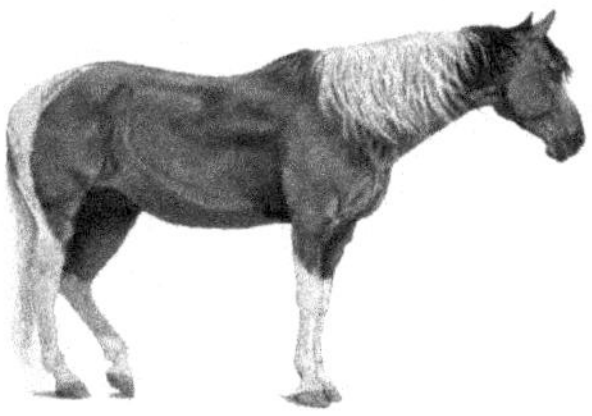

말 [mal]

rabbit

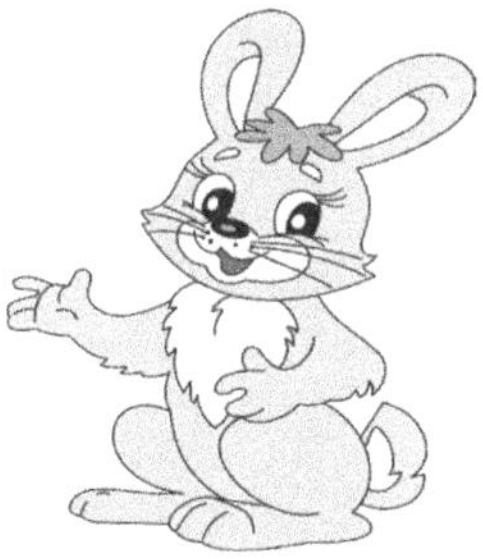

토끼 [to-kki]

dog

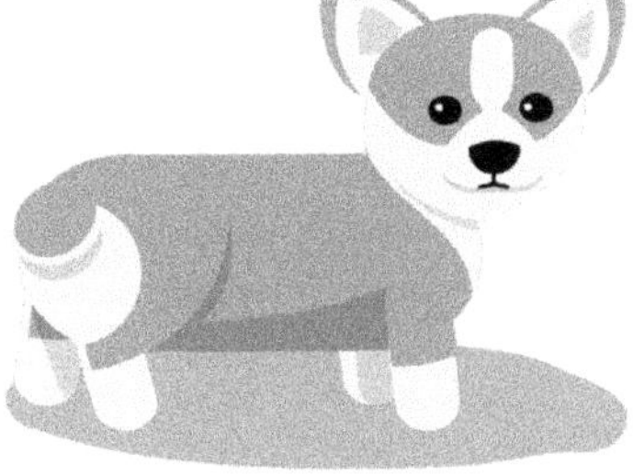

개 [gae]

cat

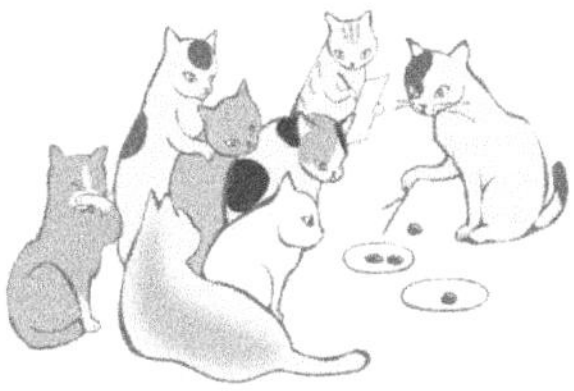

고양이 [go-yang-i]

monkey

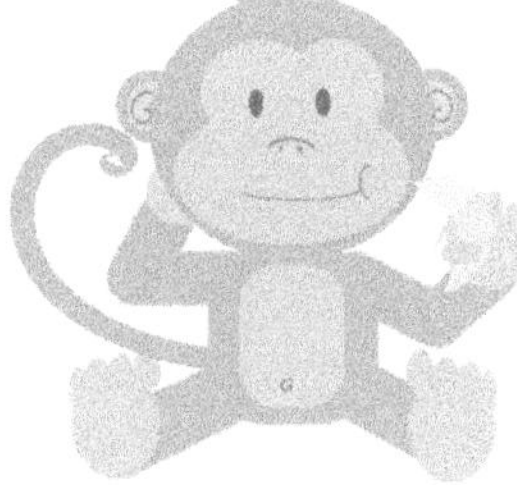

원숭이 [wŏn-sung-i]

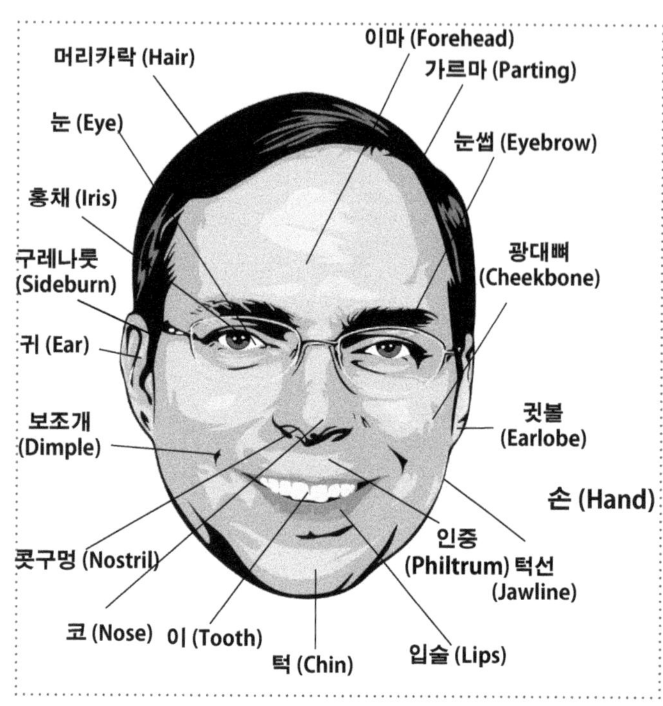
머리카락 (Hair)
이마 (Forehead)
가르마 (Parting)
눈 (Eye)
눈썹 (Eyebrow)
홍채 (Iris)
구레나룻 (Sideburn)
광대뼈 (Cheekbone)
귀 (Ear)
귓볼 (Earlobe)
보조개 (Dimple)
손 (Hand)
인중 (Philtrum)
턱선 (Jawline)
콧구멍 (Nostril)
코 (Nose)
이 (Tooth)
턱 (Chin)
입술 (Lips)

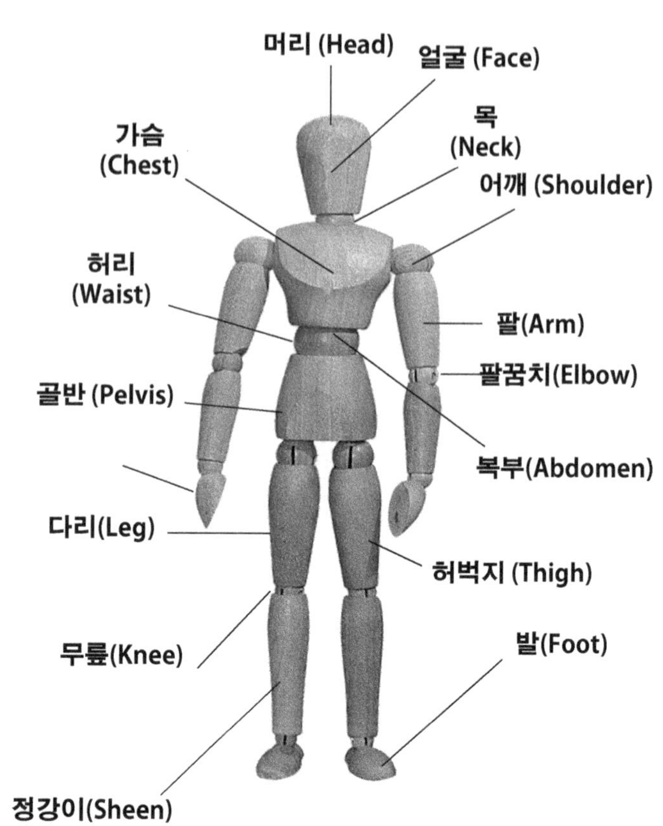
머리 (Head)
얼굴 (Face)
목 (Neck)
가슴 (Chest)
어깨 (Shoulder)
허리 (Waist)
팔(Arm)
팔꿈치(Elbow)
골반 (Pelvis)
복부(Abdomen)
다리(Leg)
허벅지 (Thigh)
무릎(Knee)
발(Foot)
정강이(Sheen)

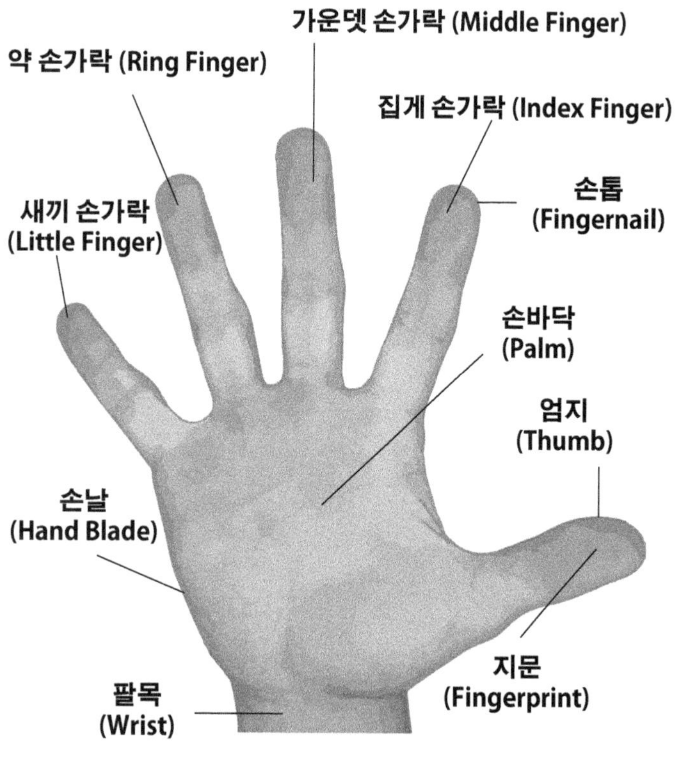
가운뎃 손가락 (Middle Finger)
약 손가락 (Ring Finger)
집게 손가락 (Index Finger)
손톱 (Fingernail)
새끼 손가락 (Little Finger)
손바닥 (Palm)
엄지 (Thumb)
손날 (Hand Blade)
지문 (Fingerprint)
팔목 (Wrist)

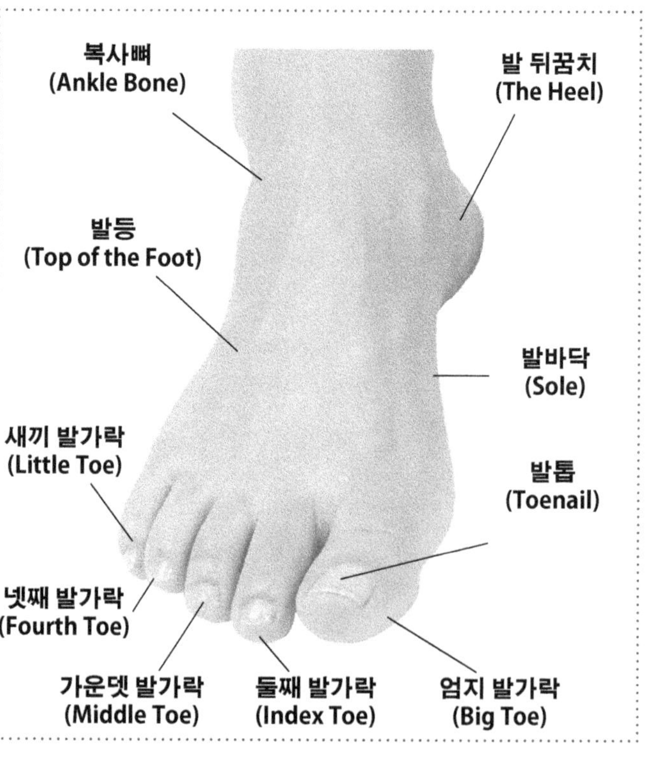
복사뼈 (Ankle Bone)
발 뒤꿈치 (The Heel)
발등 (Top of the Foot)
발바닥 (Sole)
새끼 발가락 (Little Toe)
발톱 (Toenail)
넷째 발가락 (Fourth Toe)
가운뎃 발가락 (Middle Toe)
둘째 발가락 (Index Toe)
엄지 발가락 (Big Toe)

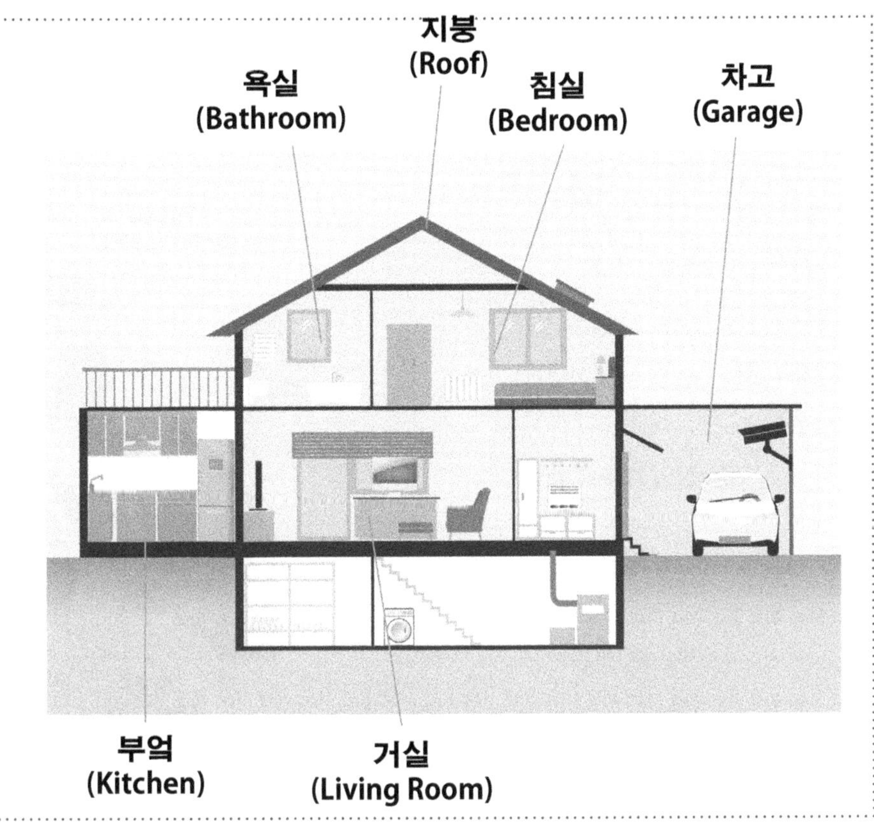

비행기 (Airplane)

버스 (Bus)

기차 (Train)

자전거 (Bicycle)

오토바이 (Motorcycle)

지하철 (Subway)

년/연도 (Year)
달/월 (Month)
날짜 (Date)
공휴일 (Holiday)
05 2016 MAY
주말 (Weekend)
주중/평일 (Weekday)
월요일 (Monday) 화요일 (Tuesday) 수요일 (Wednesday)
목요일 (Thursday) 금요일 (Friday) 토요일 (Saturday) 일요일 (Sunday)

종업원
(Waiter/Waitress)
주문서
(Order Sheet)
손님
(Customer)
찻 잔
(Tea Cup)
식탁
(Dining Table)

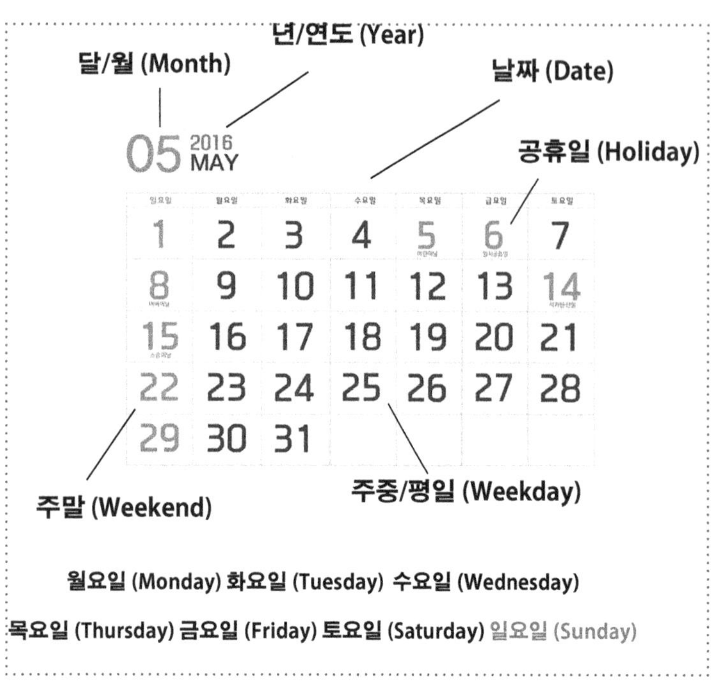

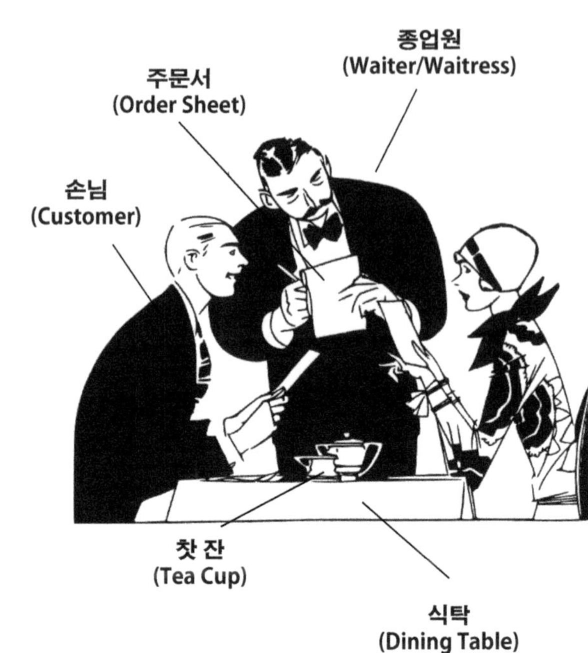

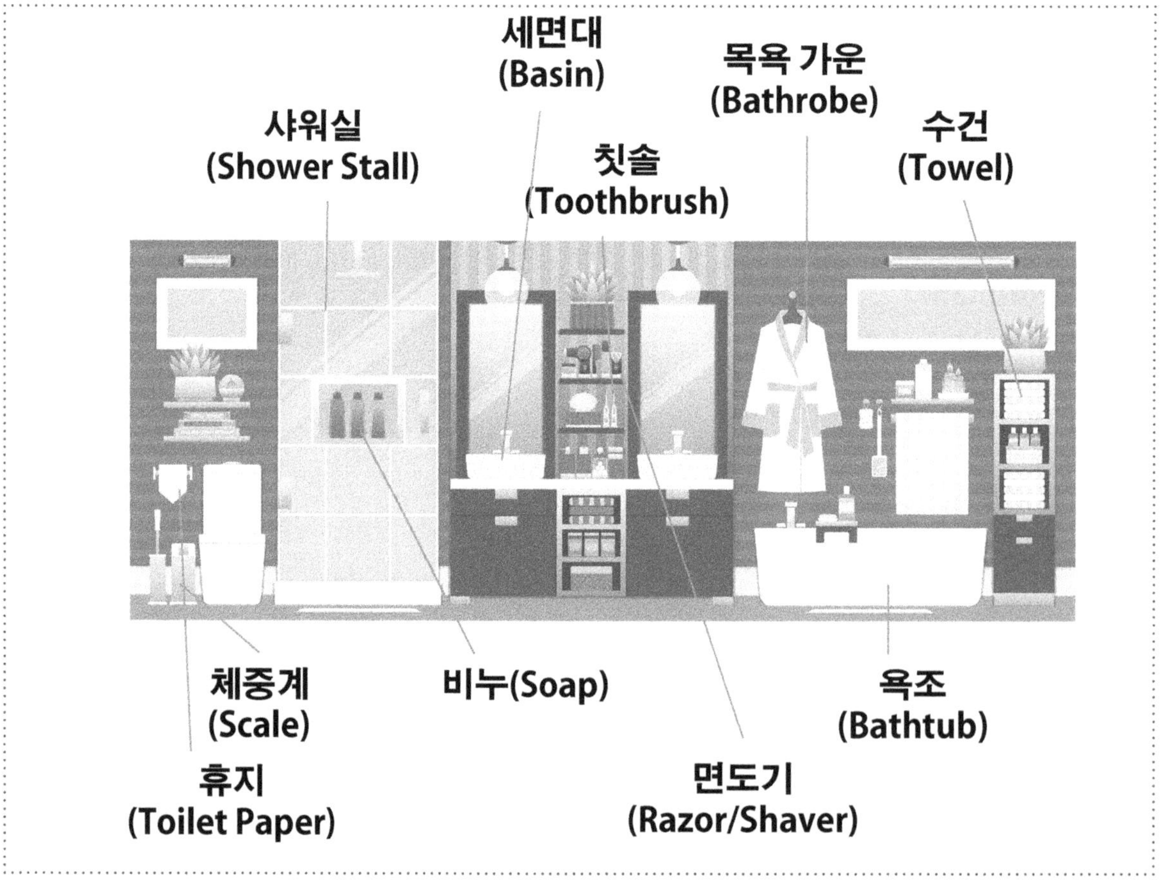

세면대
(Basin)
목욕 가운
(Bathrobe)
샤워실
(Shower Stall)
칫솔
(Toothbrush)
수건
(Towel)
체중계
(Scale)
비누(Soap)
욕조
(Bathtub)
휴지
(Toilet Paper)
면도기
(Razor/Shaver)

Fill in the blanks with appropriate Korean words.

1. 나는 (　　　) 이다.
[na-nŭn (　　　)-i-da.]
I am a (boy).

1. 하마 [ha-ma]　2. 소리 [so-ri]　3. 나비 [na-bi]　4. 소년 [so-nyŏn]　5. 사과 [sa-gwa]

2. (　　　)은 토요일이다.
[(　　　)-ŭn to-yo-il-i-da.]
(Today) is Saturday.

1. 내일 [nae-il]　2. 나 [na]　3. 시간 [shi-gan]　4. 꿈 [kkum]　5. 오늘 [o-nŭl]

3. (　　　)를 마셨다.
[(　　　)-rŭl ma-shŏt-da.]
I drank (milk).

1. 우유 [u-yu]　2. 차 [cha]　3. 물 [mul]　4. 밥 [bap]　5. 두유 [du-yu]

4. (　　　)을 씻었다.
[(　　　)-ŭl ssi-sŏt-da.]
I washed my (face).

1. 코 [ko]　2. 머리 [mŏ-ri]　3. 얼굴 [ŏl-gul]　4. 귀 [gwi]　5. 다리 [da-ri]

5. 빠른 (   )
[bba-rŭn (   )]
A fast (car).

1. 동물 [dong-mul]   2. 자동차 [ja-dong-cha]   3. 기차 [gi-cha]   4. 소 [so]   5. 길 [gil]

6. (   )을 잃어버렸다.
[(   )-ul il-o-bo-ryot-da.]
I lost the (wallet).

1. 돈 [don]   2. 길 [gil]   3. 지갑 [ji-gab]   4. 가방 [ga-bang]   5. 신발 [shin-bal]

7. (   )가 잠들었다.
[(   )-ga jam-dŭl-ot-da.]
The (baby) fell asleep.

1. 아기 [a-gi]   2. 엄마 [ŏm-ma]   3. 동생 [dong-saeng]   4. 개 [gae]   5. 새 [sae]

8. (   ) 건물
[(   ) gon-mul]
A (high) building.

1. 낮은 [na-jŭn]   2. 높은 [no-pŭn]   3. 느린 [nŭ-rin]   4. 멋진 [mŏt-jin]   5. 큰 [kŭn]

9. (   )을 읽고있다.
[(   )-ŭl il-kko-it-da.]
I am reading a (book).

1. 잡지 [jap-ji]   2. 책 [chaek]   3. 소설 [so-sŏl]   4. 소리 [so-ri]   5. 기회 [gi-hoe]

10. 어려운 (   )
[ŏ-ryo-un (   )]
A difficult (problem).

1. 일 [il]   2. 바람 [ba-ram]   3. 문제 [mun-je]   4. 그림 [gŭ-rim]   5. 책 [chaek]

11. 자동차가 (   ).
[ja-dong-cha-ga (   ).]
The car (stopped).

1. 멈췄다 [mŏm-chwŏt-da]   2. 먹다 [mŏk-da]   3. 입다 [ip-da]
4. 했다 [haet-da]   5. 달렸다 [dal-lyŏt-da]

12. (   )가 울고있다.
[(   ) ga ul-go-it-da.]
A (girl) is crying.

1. 소녀 [so-nyŏ]   2. 아기 [a-gi]   3. 강아지 [gang-a-ji]   4. 다리 [da-ri]   5. 소 [so]

13. 내일은 내 (   )이다.
[nae-il-ŭn nae (   ) i-da.]
Tomorrow is my (birthday).

1. 생선 [saeng-sŏn]   2. 시험 [shi-hŏm]   3. 꿈 [kkum]   4. 생일 [saeng-il]   5. 길 [gil]

14. (   )가 재밌었다.
[(   ) ga jae-mi-ssŏt-da.]
(Movie) was fun.

1. 야구 [ya-gu]   2. 영화 [yŏng-hwa]   3. 노래 [no-rae]
4. 이야기 [i-ya-gi]   5. 만화 [man-hwa]

15. (   ) 좀 주세요.

[(   ) jom ju-se-yo.]

Please give me some (water).

1. 돈 [don]   2. 김 [gim]   3. 불 [bul]   4. 술 [sul]   5. 물 [mul]

16. (   )가 좋다.

[(   ) ga jot-da.]

The (weather) is good.

1. 기차 [gi-cha]   2. 소리 [so-ri]   3. 날씨 [nal-ssi]   4. 새 [sae]   5. 사과 [sa-gwa]

17. (   )을 먹어라.

[(   ) ŭl mŏk-o-ra.]

Have (lunch).

1. 아침 [a-chim]   2. 저녁 [jŏ-nyok]   3. 간식 [gan-sik]   4. 점심 [jŏm-sim]   5. 밥 [bap]

18. (   )을 듣는다.

[(   ) ŭl dŭt-nŭn-da.]

I listen to (music).

1. 음악 [ŭm-ak]   2. 춤 [chum]   3. 말 [mal]   4. 꿈 [kkum]   5. 그림 [gŭ-rim]

19. (   )이 부족하다.

[(   ) i bu-jok-ha-da.]

There is not enough (time).

1. 힘 [him]   2. 손 [son]   3. 시간 [shi-gan]   4. 사람 [sa-ram]   5. 음식 [ŭm-sik]

20. 규칙적인 (   )
[gyu-chik-jok-in (   )]
Regular (exercise).

1. 공부 [gong-bu]   2. 일 [il]   3. 잠 [jam]   4. 일기 [il-gi]   5. 운동 [un-dong]

21. (   ) 요리.
[(   ) yo-ri.]
(Delicious) meal.

1. 맛있는 [ma-shit-nŭn]   2. 멋있는 [mŏ-shit-nŭn]   3. 빠른 [bba-rŭn]
4. 큰 [kŭn]   5. 느린 [nŭ-rin]

22. (   ) 인생
[(   ) in-saeng]
(Busy) life.

1. 바쁜 [ba-ppŭn]   2. 이른 [i-rŭn]   3. 힘든 [him-dŭn]   4. 꿈 [kkum]   5. 오늘 [o-nŭl]

23. (   ) 도서관
[(   ) do-sŏ-gwan]
(Quiet) library

1. 큰 [kŭn]   2. 조용한 [jo-yong-han]   3. 먼 [mŏn]   4. 깊은 [gi-pŭn]   5. 센 [sen]

24. 차가운 (   )
[cha-ga-un (   )]
Cold (ice)

1. 기름 [gi-rŭm]   2. 얼음 [ŏ-rŭm]   3. 이름 [i-rŭm]   4. 시름 [shi-rŭm]   5. 거름 [gŏ-rŭm]

25. (   ) 김치

[(   ) kim-chi]

(Spicy) Kim-chi.

1. 단 [dan]   2. 쓴 [ssŭn]   3. 매운 [mae-un]   4. 짠 [jjan]   5. 미운 [mi-un]

ANSWER KEY

1. 4 소년 [so-nyŏn]
2. 5 오늘 [o-nŭl]
3. 1 우유 [u-yu]
4. 3 얼굴 [ol-gul]
5. 2 자동차 [ja-dong-cha]
6. 3 지갑 [ji-gab]
7. 1 아기 [a-gi]
8. 2 높은 [no-pŭn]
9. 2 책 [chaek]
10. 3 문제 [mun-je]
11. 1 멈췄다 [mom-chwot-da]
12. 1 소녀 [so-nyo]
13. 4 생일 [saeng-il]
14. 2 영화 [yong-hwa]
15. 5 물 [mul]
16. 3 날씨 [nal-ssi]
17. 4 점심 [jom-sim]
18. 1 음악 [ŭm-ak]
19. 3 시간 [shi-gan]
20. 5 운동 [un-dong]
21. 1 맛있는 [ma-shit-nŭn]
22. 1 바쁜 [ba-ppŭn]
23. 2 조용한 [jo-yong-han]
24. 2 얼음 [ol-ŭm]
25. 3 매운 [mae-un]

MATCHING HOMONYMS

Some words sound the same but have more than one meaning.
Choose the appropriate word and write it in the box provided.

사과 [sa-gwa]
말 [mal]
짐 [jib]
눈 [nun]
미리 [mi-ri]
소리 [so-ri]
김 [gim]
종이 [jong-i]
손 [son]

horse — language/word

snow  — eye

laver  — steam

탈
[tal]
차
[cha]
도리
[do-ri]
다리
[da-ri]
잠수
[jam-su]
하나
[ha-na]
다리
[da-ri]
궁
[gung]
사과
[sa-gwa]
leg
bridge
apology
SORRY
apple
year
Happy
New Year
sun
car
tea

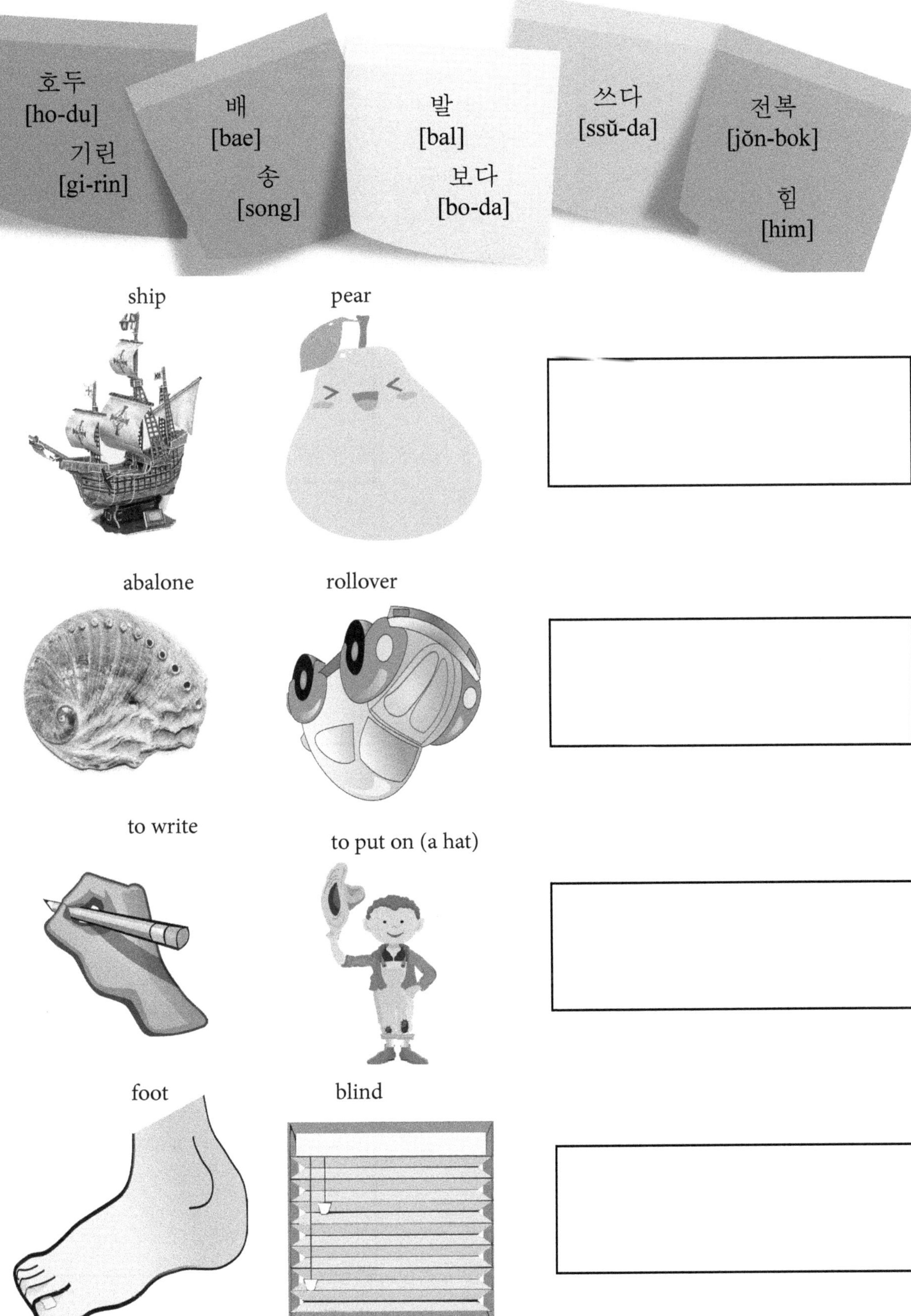
호두
[ho-du]
기린
[gi-rin]
배
[bae]
송
[song]
발
[bal]
보다
[bo-da]
쓰다
[ssŭ-da]
전복
[jŏn-bok]
힘
[him]
ship
pear
abalone
rollover
to write
to put on (a hat)
foot
blind

가루
[ga-ru]
세로
[se-ro]
침
[chim]
시간
[shi-gan]
성
[sŏng]
가방
[ga-bang]
절
[jŏl]
기상
[gi-sang]
길
[gil]
bow
temple
family name
castle
KIM
SMITH
spit/saliva
needle/accupuncutre
to wake up
weather conditions

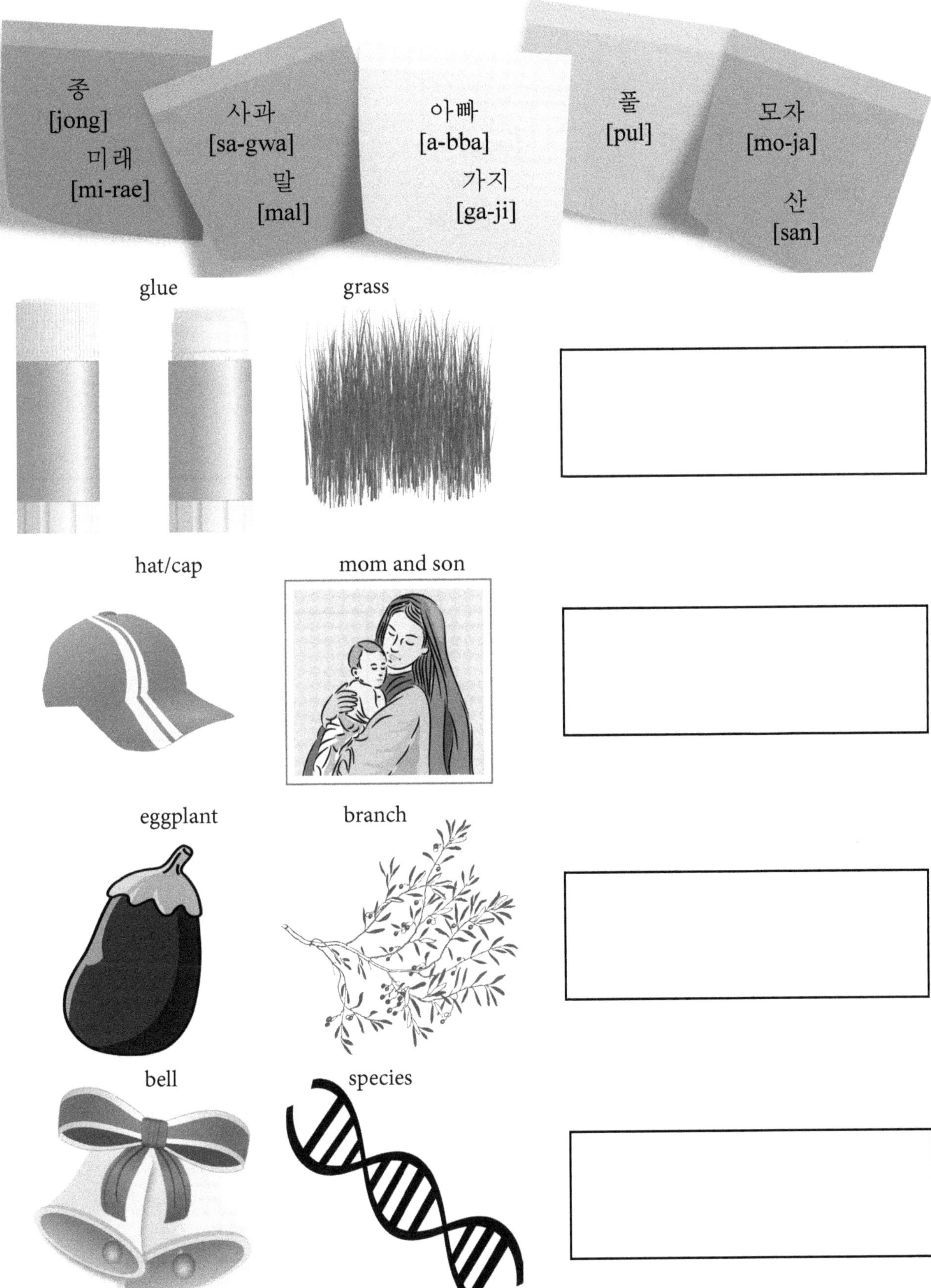
종
[jong]
미래
[mi-rae]
사과
[sa-gwa]
말
[mal]
아빠
[a-bba]
가지
[ga-ji]
풀
[pul]
모자
[mo-ja]
산
[san]
glue
grass
hat/cap
mom and son
eggplant
branch
bell
species

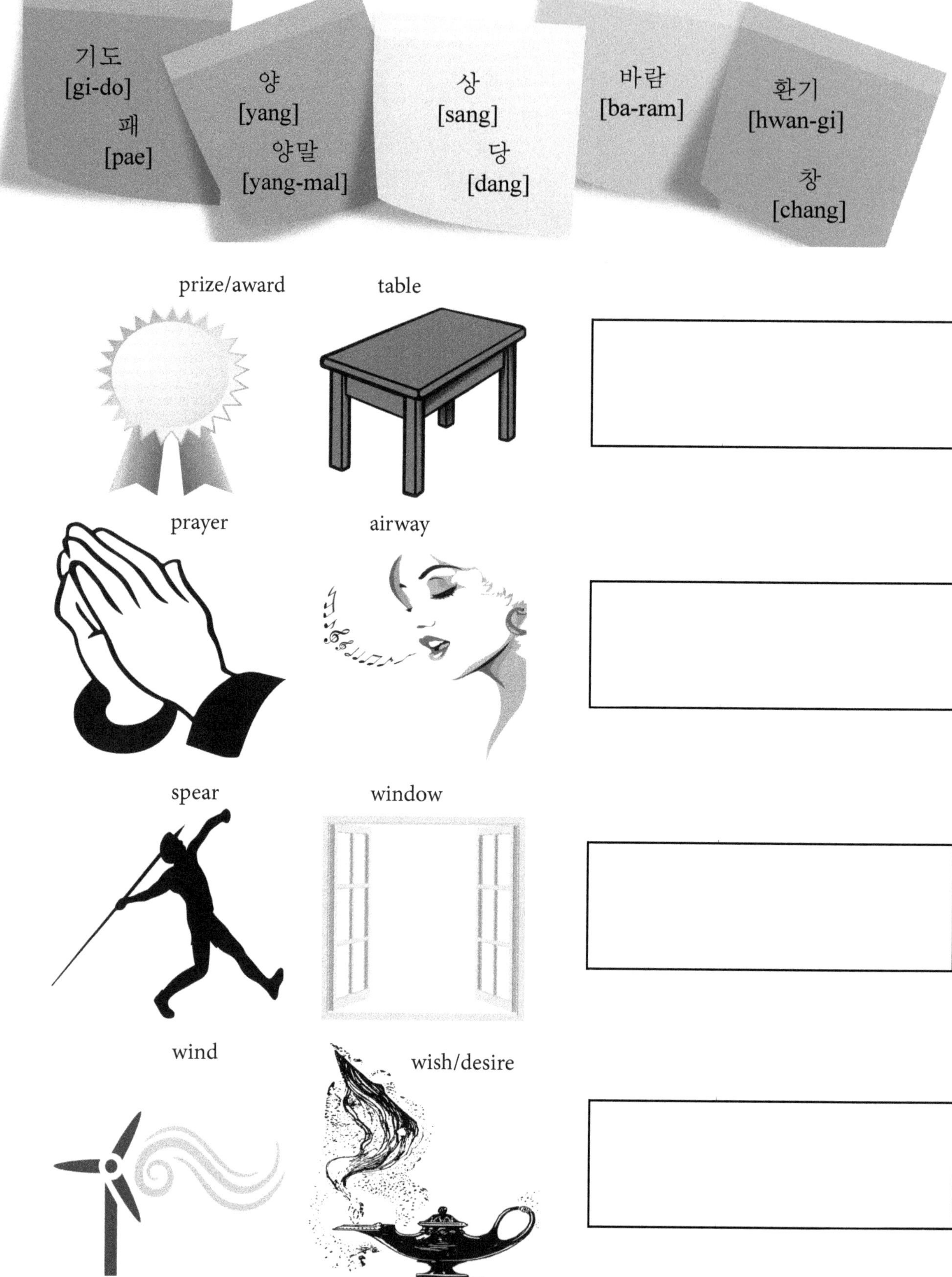
기도
[gi-do]
패
[pae]
양
[yang]
양말
[yang-mal]
상
[sang]
당
[dang]
바람
[ba-ram]
환기
[hwan-gi]
창
[chang]
prize/award
table
prayer
airway
spear
window
wind
wish/desire

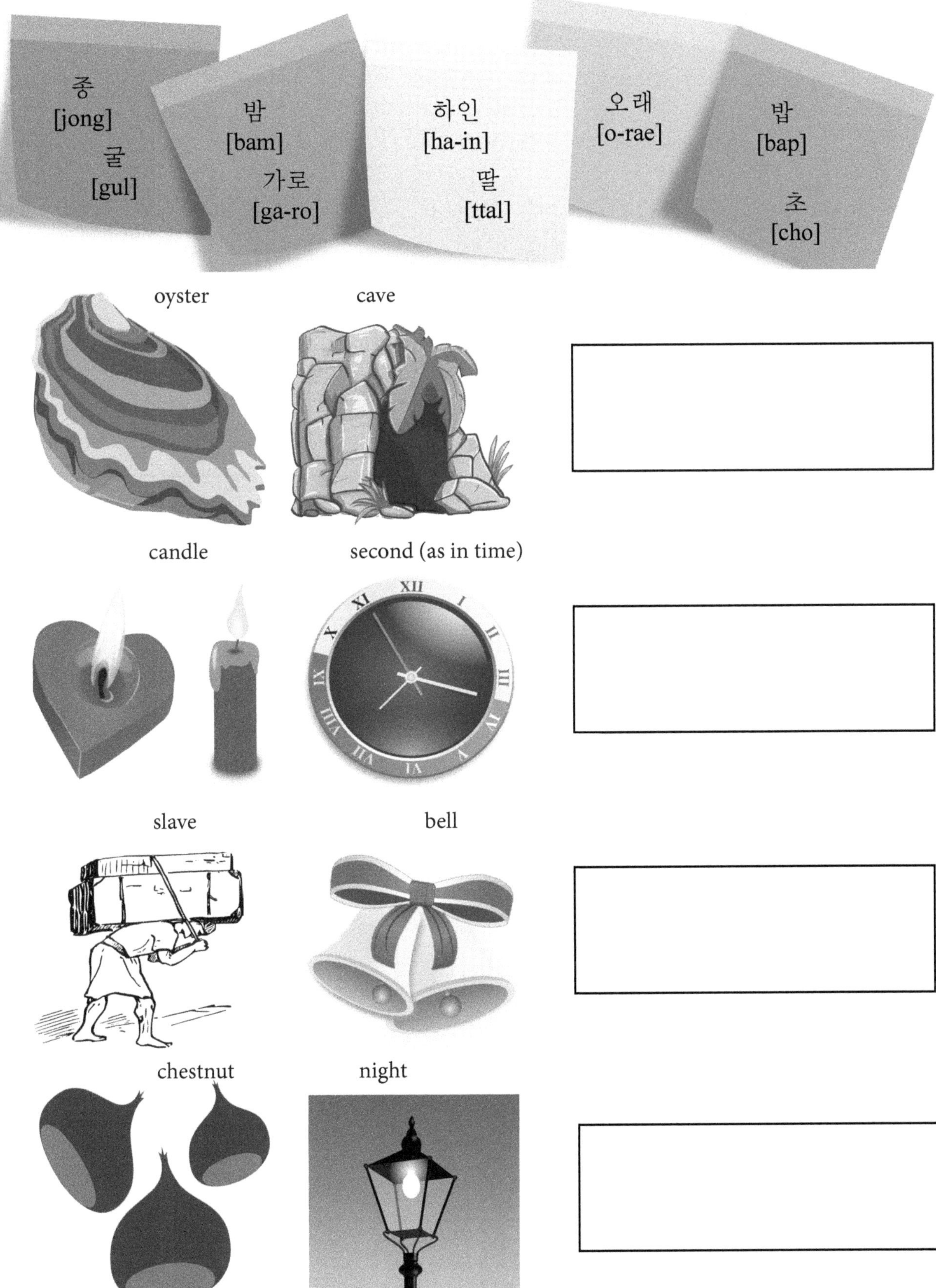

종
[jong]
굴
[gul]
밤
[bam]
가로
[ga-ro]
하인
[ha-in]
딸
[ttal]
오래
[o-rae]
밥
[bap]
초
[cho]
oyster
cave
candle
second (as in time)
slave
bell
chestnut
night

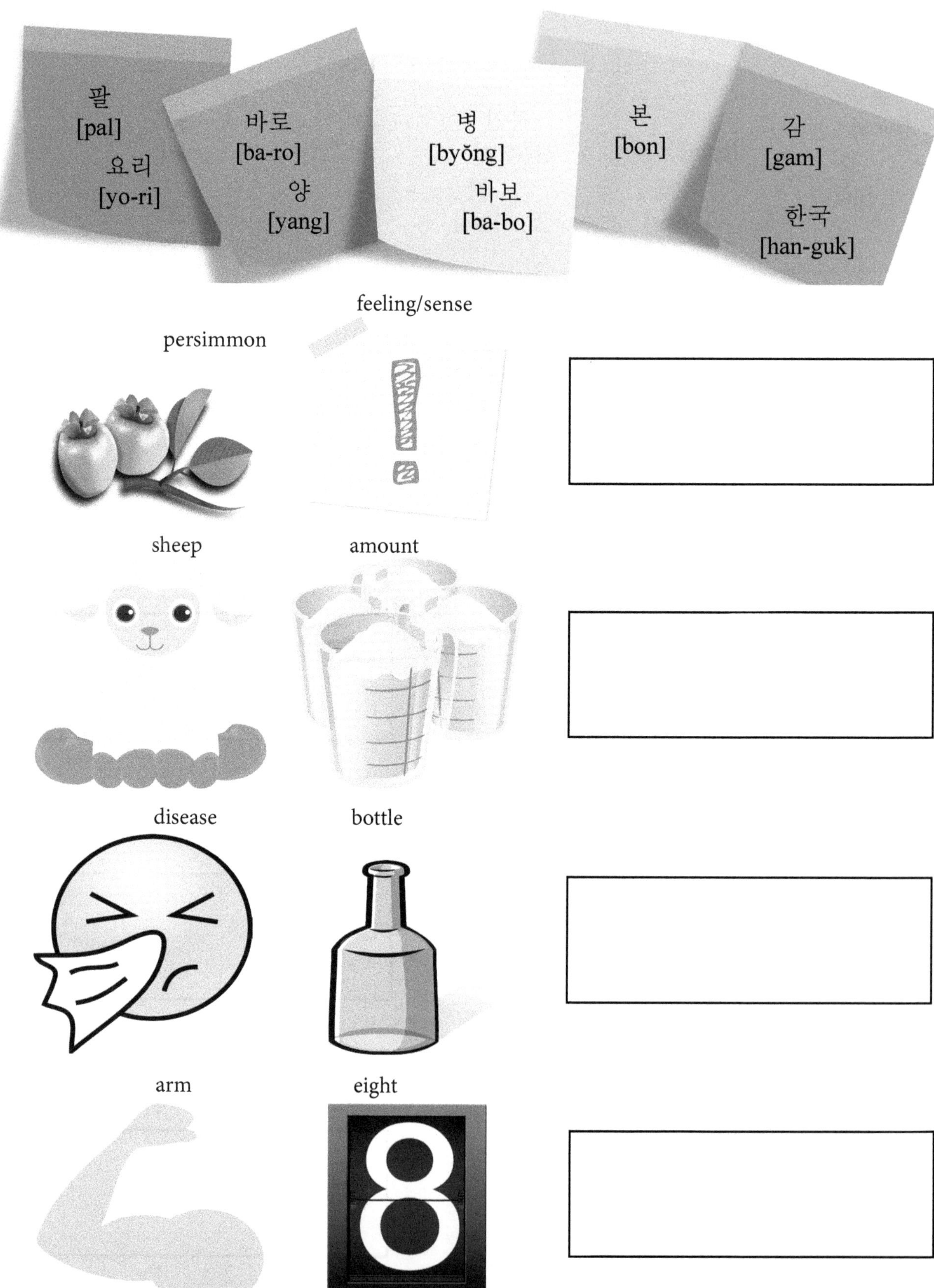
팔
[pal]
요리
[yo-ri]
바로
[ba-ro]
양
[yang]
병
[byŏng]
바보
[ba-bo]
본
[bon]
감
[gam]
한국
[han-guk]
persimmon
feeling/sense
sheep
amount
disease
bottle
arm
eight

신
[shin]
열
[yŏl]
두부
[du-bu]
박
[bak]
이
[i]
뱀
[baem]
면
[myŏn]
생기
[saeng-gi]
모래
[mo-rae]
two
tooth
ten
fever
10
side (of a square)
noodle
shoe
god
THINK
GOD

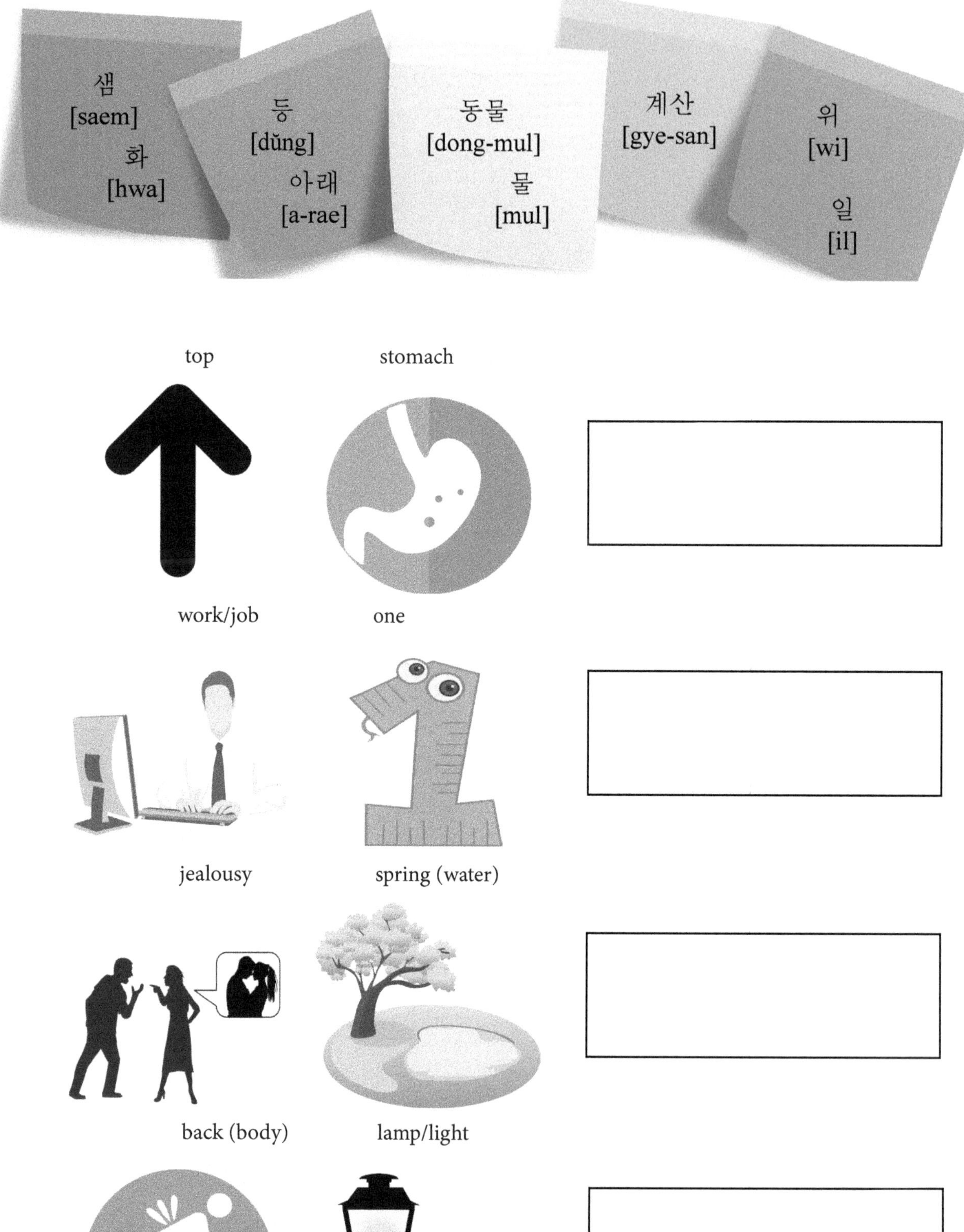
샘
[saem]
화
[hwa]
등
[dŭng]
아래
[a-rae]
동물
[dong-mul]
물
[mul]
계산
[gye-san]
위
[wi]
일
[il]
top
stomach
work/job
one
jealousy
spring (water)
back (body)
lamp/light

ANSWER KEY

horse
text message
말 [mal]
snow
eye
눈 [nun]
laver
steam
김 [gim]
leg
bridge
다리 [da-ri]
apology
SORRY
apple
사과 [sa-gwa]
year
Happy New Year
sun
해 [hae]
car
tea
차 [cha]
ship
pear
배 [bae]
abalone
rollover
전복 [jŏn-bok]
to write
to put on (a hat)
쓰다 [ssu-da]
foot
blind
발 [bal]
bow
temple
절 [jŏl]
family name
KIM
SMITH
castle
성 [sŏng]
spit/saliva
needle/accupuncutre
침 [chim]
to wake up
weather conditions
기상 [gi-sang]

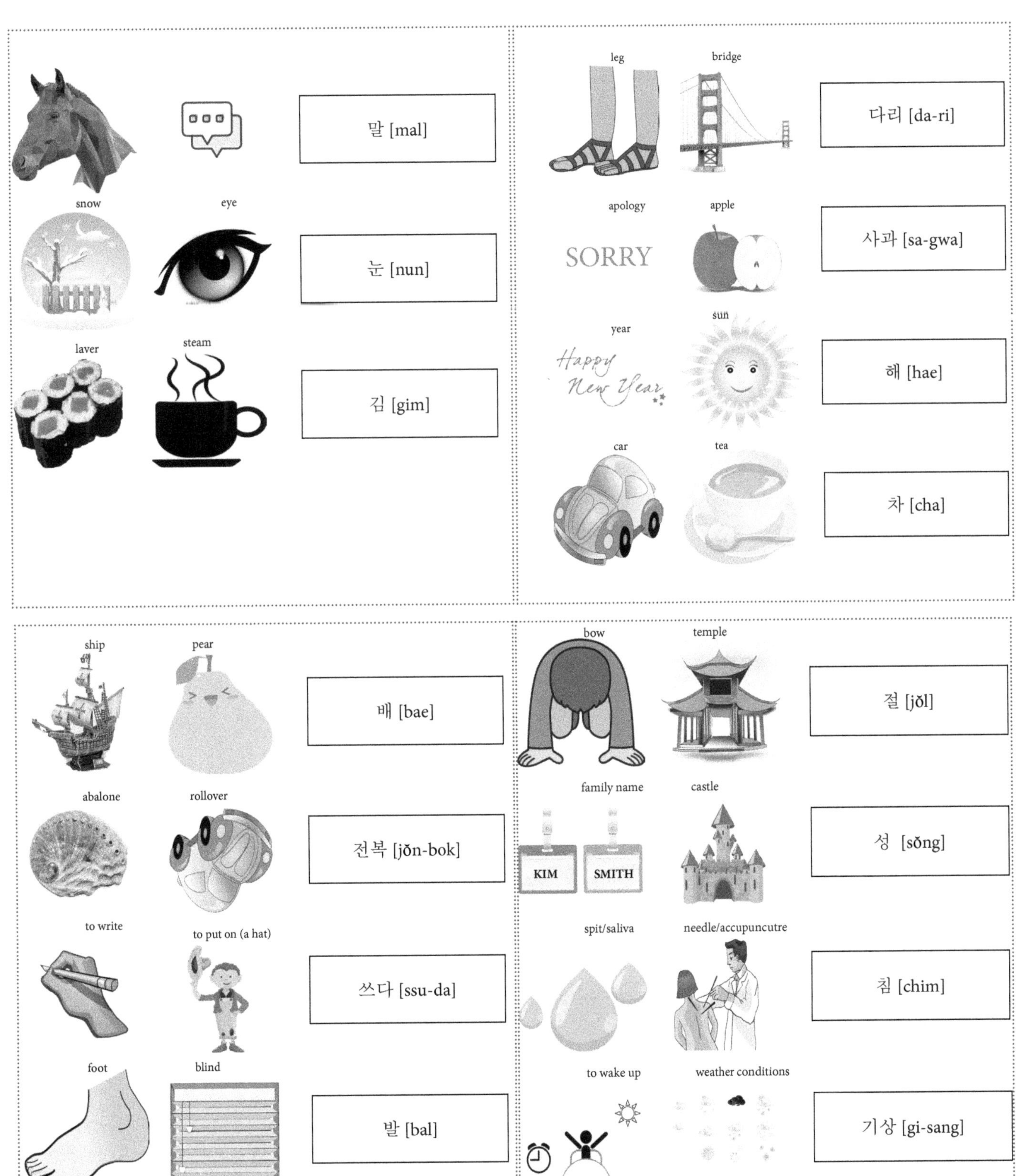

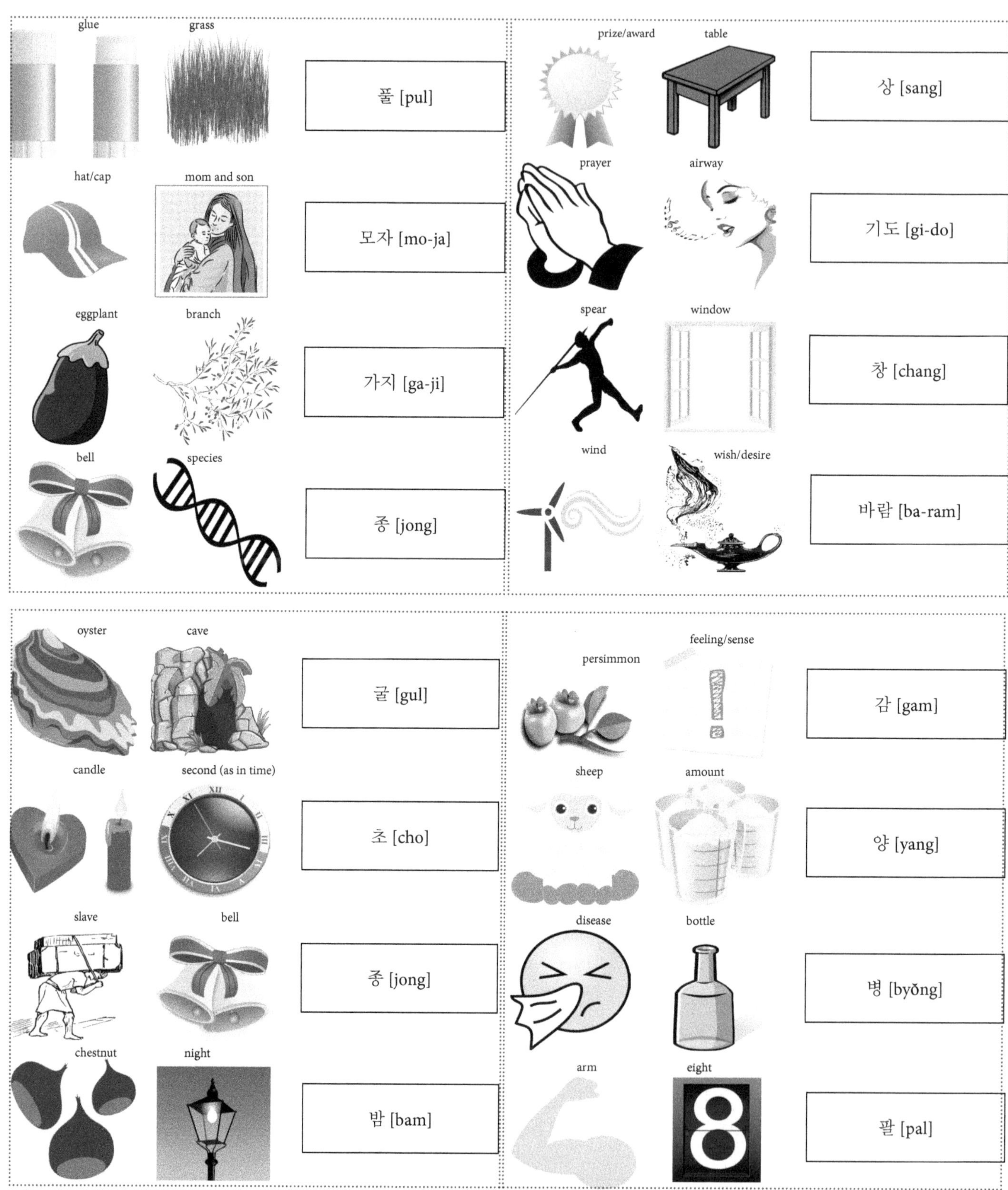
glue
grass
풀 [pul]
hat/cap
mom and son
모자 [mo-ja]
eggplant
branch
가지 [ga-ji]
bell
species
종 [jong]
prize/award
table
상 [sang]
prayer
airway
기도 [gi-do]
spear
window
창 [chang]
wind
wish/desire
바람 [ba-ram]
oyster
cave
굴 [gul]
candle
second (as in time)
초 [cho]
slave
bell
종 [jong]
chestnut
night
밤 [bam]
persimmon
feeling/sense
감 [gam]
sheep
amount
양 [yang]
disease
bottle
병 [byŏng]
arm
eight
팔 [pal]

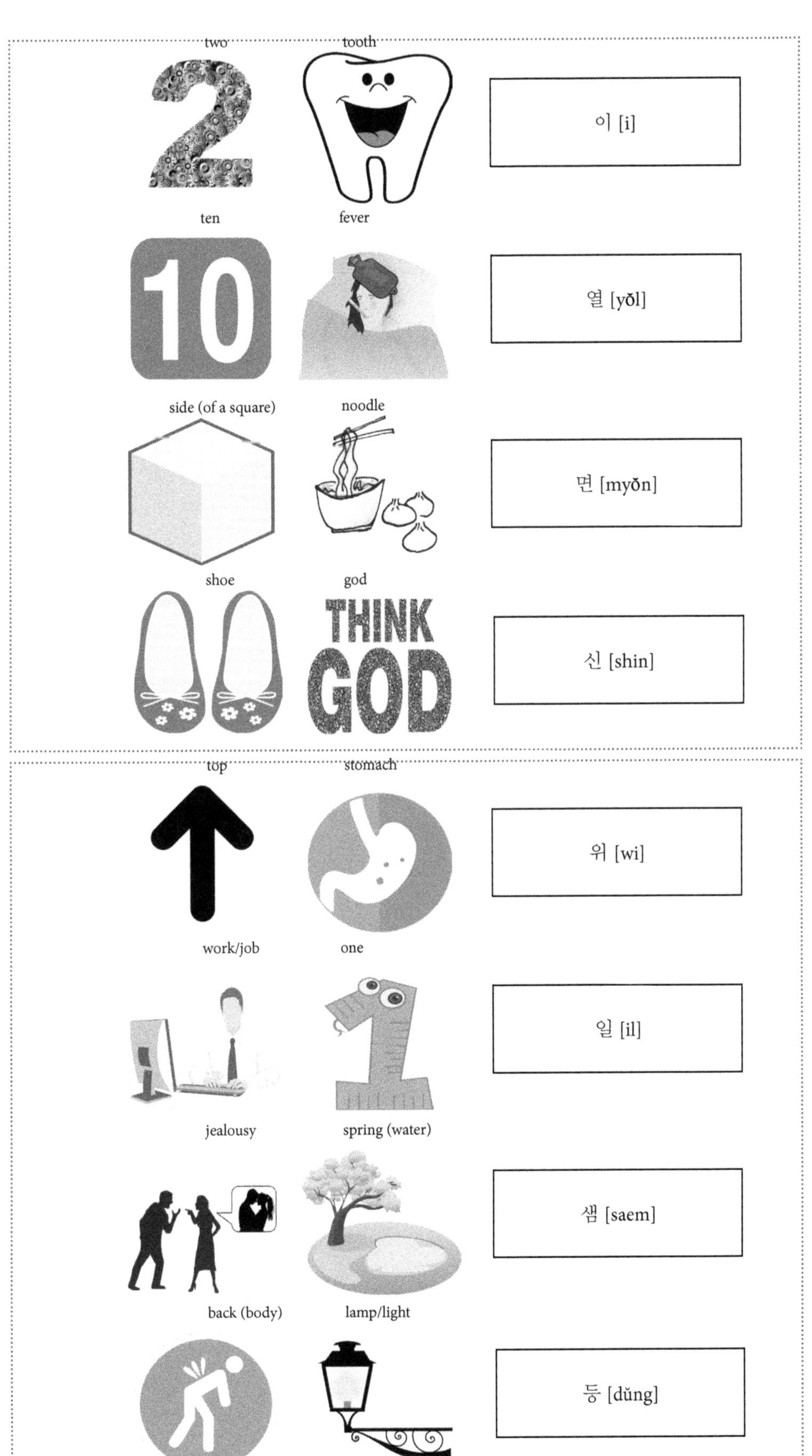
two
tooth
이 [i]
ten
fever
열 [yŏl]
side (of a square)
noodle
면 [myŏn]
shoe
god
THINK
GOD
신 [shin]
top
stomach
위 [wi]
work/job
one
일 [il]
jealousy
spring (water)
샘 [saem]
back (body)
lamp/light
등 [dŭng]

Some words sound the same but have more than one meaning.
Choose the appropriate word and write it in the box provided.

기쁨 [gi-bbŭm] ○	○ 분노 [bun-no]
화 [hwa] ○	○ 감정 [gam-jŏng]
느낌 [nŭ-kkim] ○	○ 인간 [in-gan]
말 [mal] ○	○ 즐거움 [jŭl-gŏ-um]
사람 [sa-ram] ○	○ 언어 [ŏn-o]

책
[chaek]

공부
[gong-bu]

선생님
[sŏn-saeng-nim]

학교
[hak-gyo]

진짜
[jin-jja]

연기
[yŏn-gi]

교육
[gyo-yuk]

정말
[jŏng-mal]

김
[gim]

학당
[hak-dang]

도서
[do-sŏ]

교사
[gyo-sa]

해 [hae]	물고기 [mul-go-gi]
목소리 [mok-so-ri]	미소 [mi-so]
생선 [saeng-sŏn]	음성 [ŭm-song]
웃음 [u-sŭm]	태양 [tae-yang]
친구 [chin-gu]	훈련 [hun-ryŏn]
연습 [yŏn-sŭp]	동무 [dong-mu]

고민 [go-min]	○	○	구두 [gu-du]
치아 [chi-a]	○	○	아버지 [a-bŏ-ji]
신발 [shin-bal]	○	○	현재 [hyŏn-jae]
아빠 [a-bba]	○	○	이빨 [i-ppal]
어린이 [ŏ-rin-i]	○	○	아이 [a-i]
지금 [ji-gŭm]	○	○	걱정 [gŏk-jŏng]

ANSWER KEY

기쁨
[gi-bbŭm]
화
[hwa]
느낌
[nŭ-kkim]
말
[mal]
사람
[sa-ram]
분노
[bun-no]
감정
[gam-jŏng]
인간
[in-gan]
즐거움
[jul-gŏ-um]
언어
[ŏn-o]
책
[chaek]
공부
[gong-bu]
선생님
[sŏn-saeng-nim]
학교
[hak-gyo]
진짜
[jin-jja]
연기
[yŏn-gi]
교육
[gyo-yuk]
정말
[jong-mal]
김
[gim]
학당
[hak-dang]
도서
[do-sŏ]
교사
[gyo-sa]
해
[hae]
목소리
[mok-so-ri]
생선
[saeng-sŏn]
웃음
[u-sŭm]
친구
[chin-gu]
연습
[yŏn-sŭp]
물고기
[mul-go-gi]
미소
[mi-so]
음성
[ŭm-sŏng]
태양
[tae-yang]
훈련
[hun-ryŏn]
동무
[dong-mu]
고민
[go-min]
치아
[chi-a]
신발
[shin-bal]
아빠
[a-bba]
어린이
[ŏ-rin-i]
지금
[ji-gŭm]
구두
[gu-du]
아버지
[a-bŏ-ji]
현재
[hyŏn-jae]
이빨
[i-ppal]
아이
[a-i]
걱정
[gŏk-jŏng]

KOREAN VOCAB
WORKBOOK

MATCHING ANTONYMS

Some words sound the same but have more than one meaning.
Choose the appropriate word and write it in the box provided.

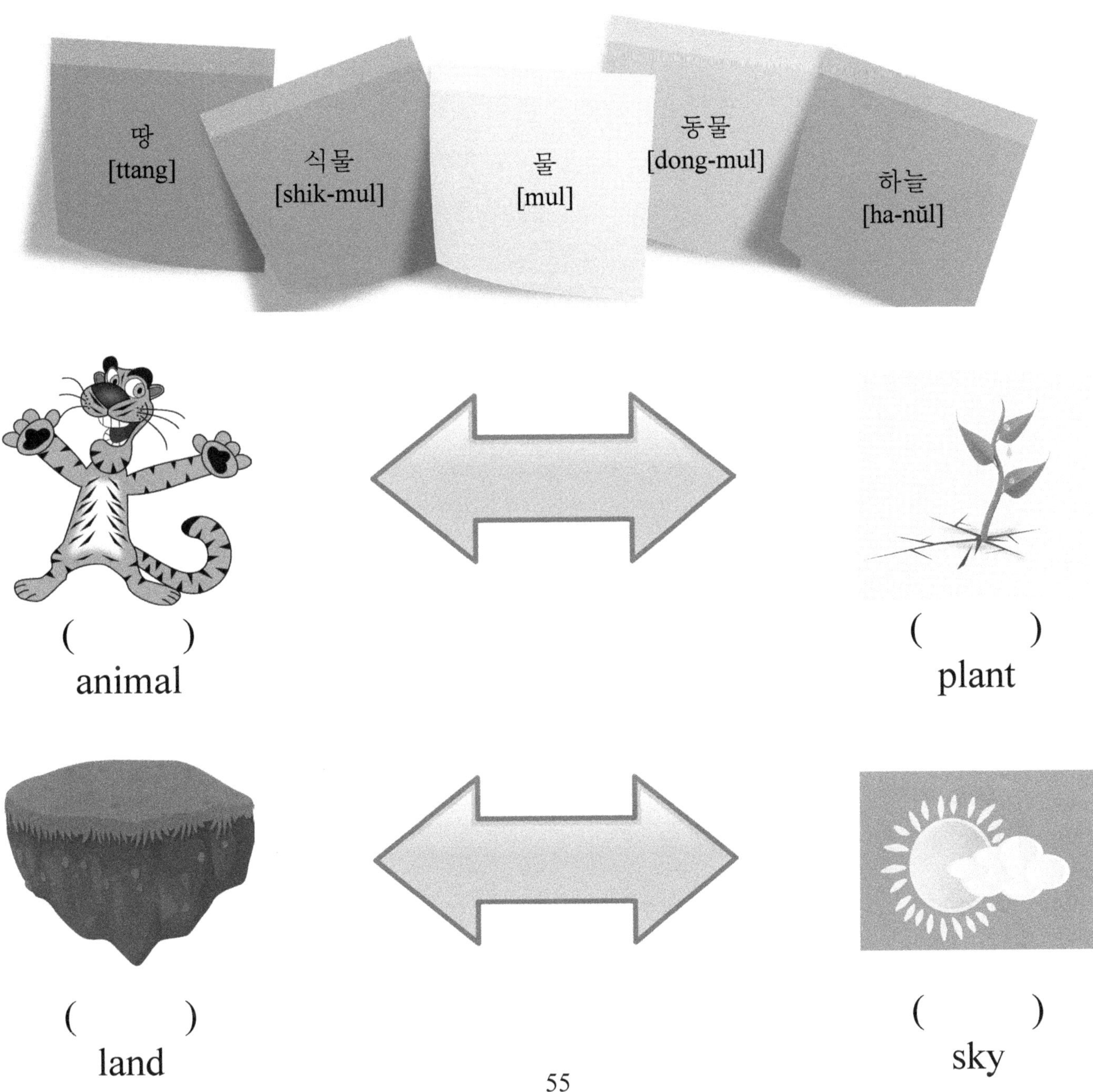

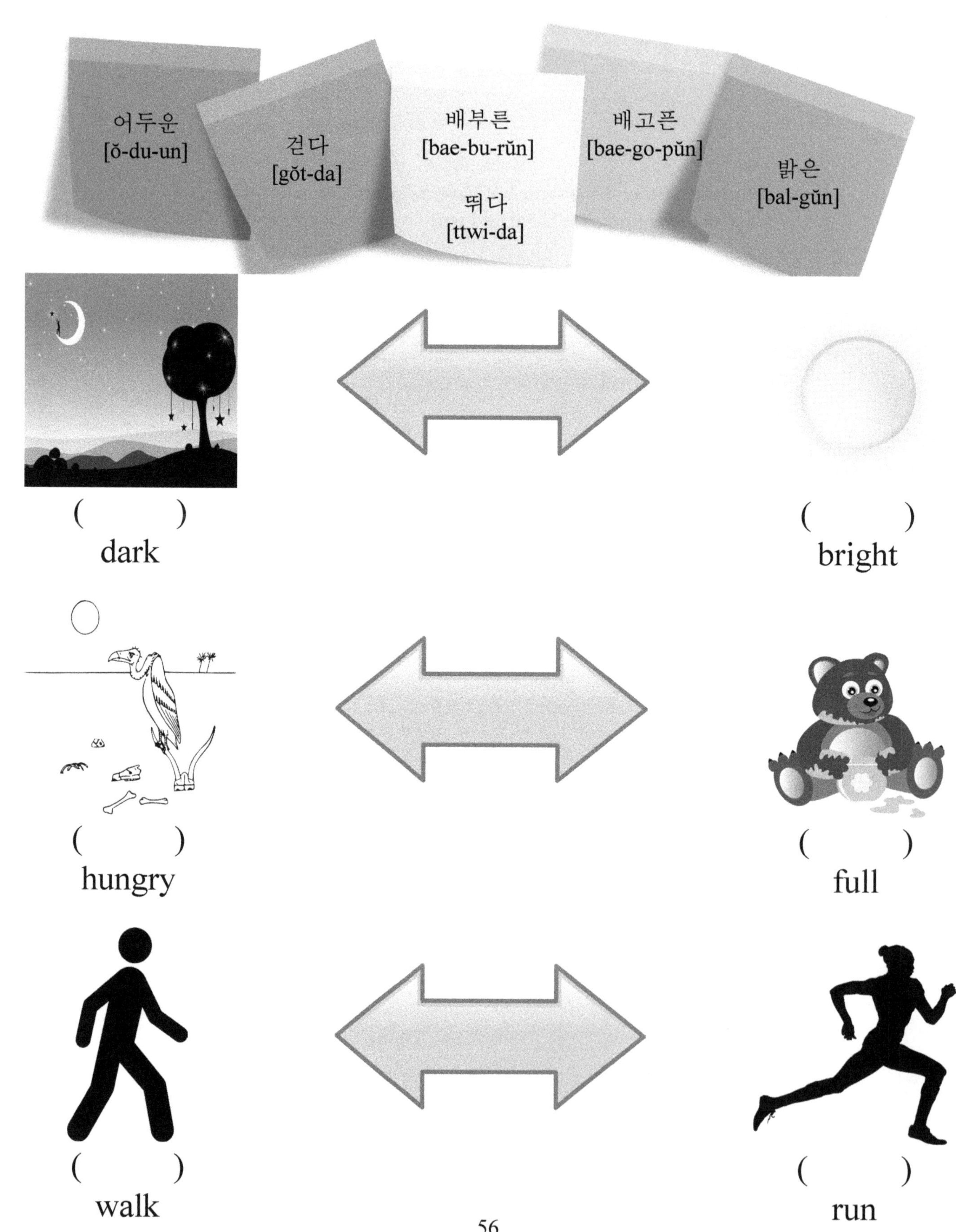

어두운
[ŏ-du-un]
걷다
[gŏt-da]
배부른
[bae-bu-rŭn]
뛰다
[ttwi-da]
배고픈
[bae-go-pŭn]
밝은
[bal-gŭn]
( )
dark
( )
bright
( )
hungry
( )
full
( )
walk
( )
run

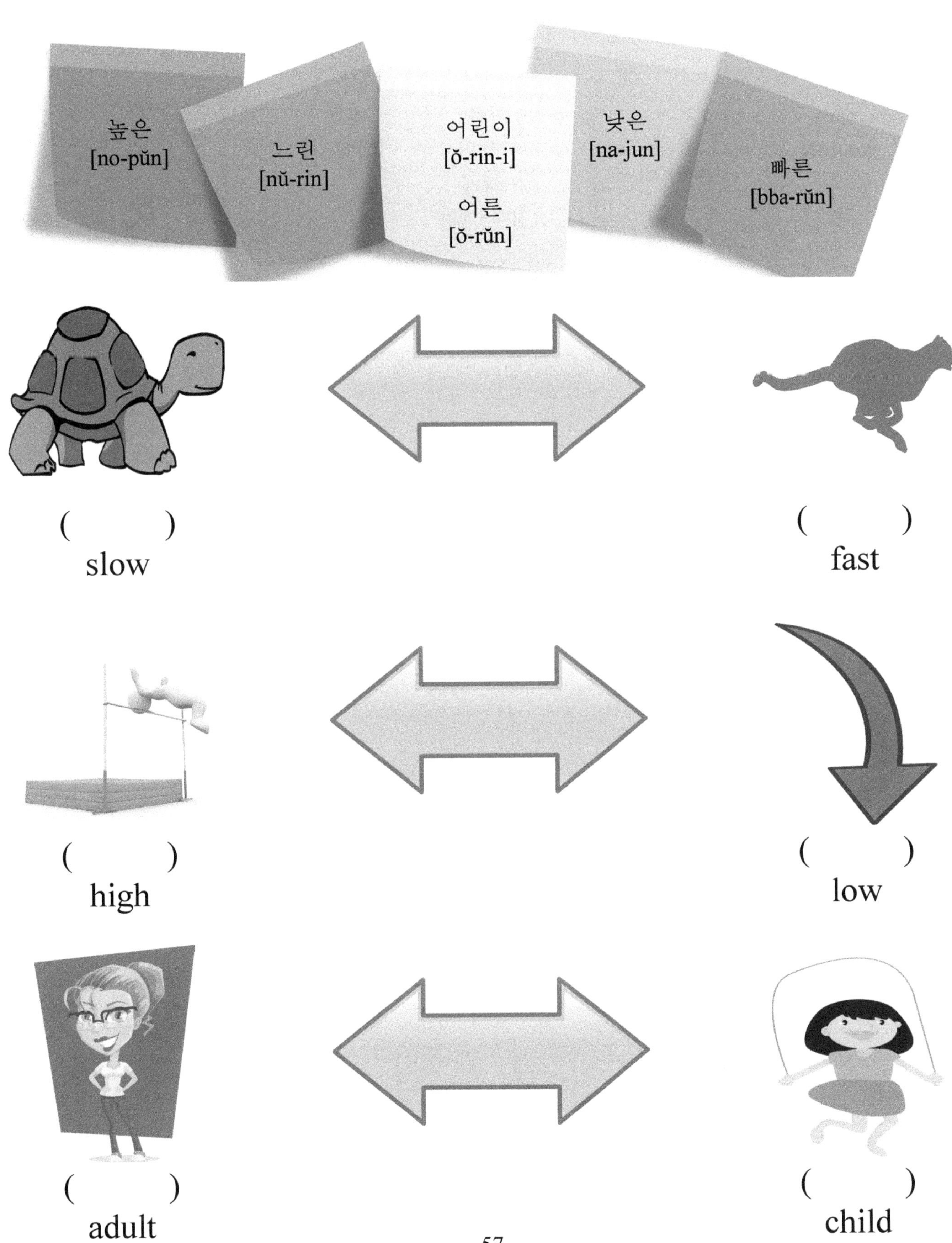

높은
[no-pŭn]
느린
[nŭ-rin]
어린이
[ŏ-rin-i]
어른
[ŏ-rŭn]
낮은
[na-jun]
빠른
[bba-rŭn]
( )
slow
( )
fast
( )
high
( )
low
( )
adult
( )
child

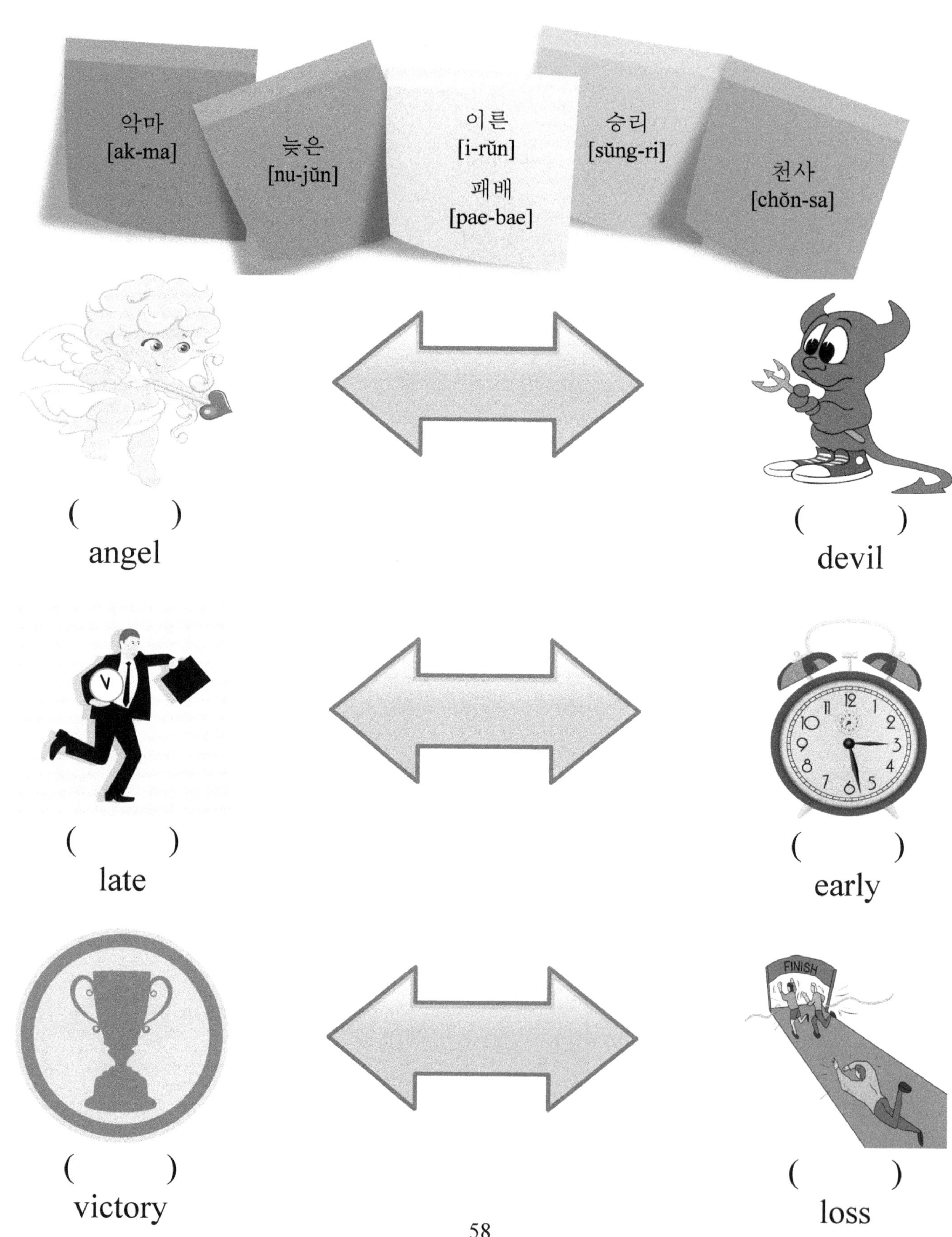

악마
[ak-ma]
늦은
[nu-jŭn]
이른
[i-rŭn]
패배
[pae-bae]
승리
[sŭng-ri]
천사
[chŏn-sa]
(   )
angel
(   )
devil
(   )
late
(   )
early
(   )
victory
(   )
loss

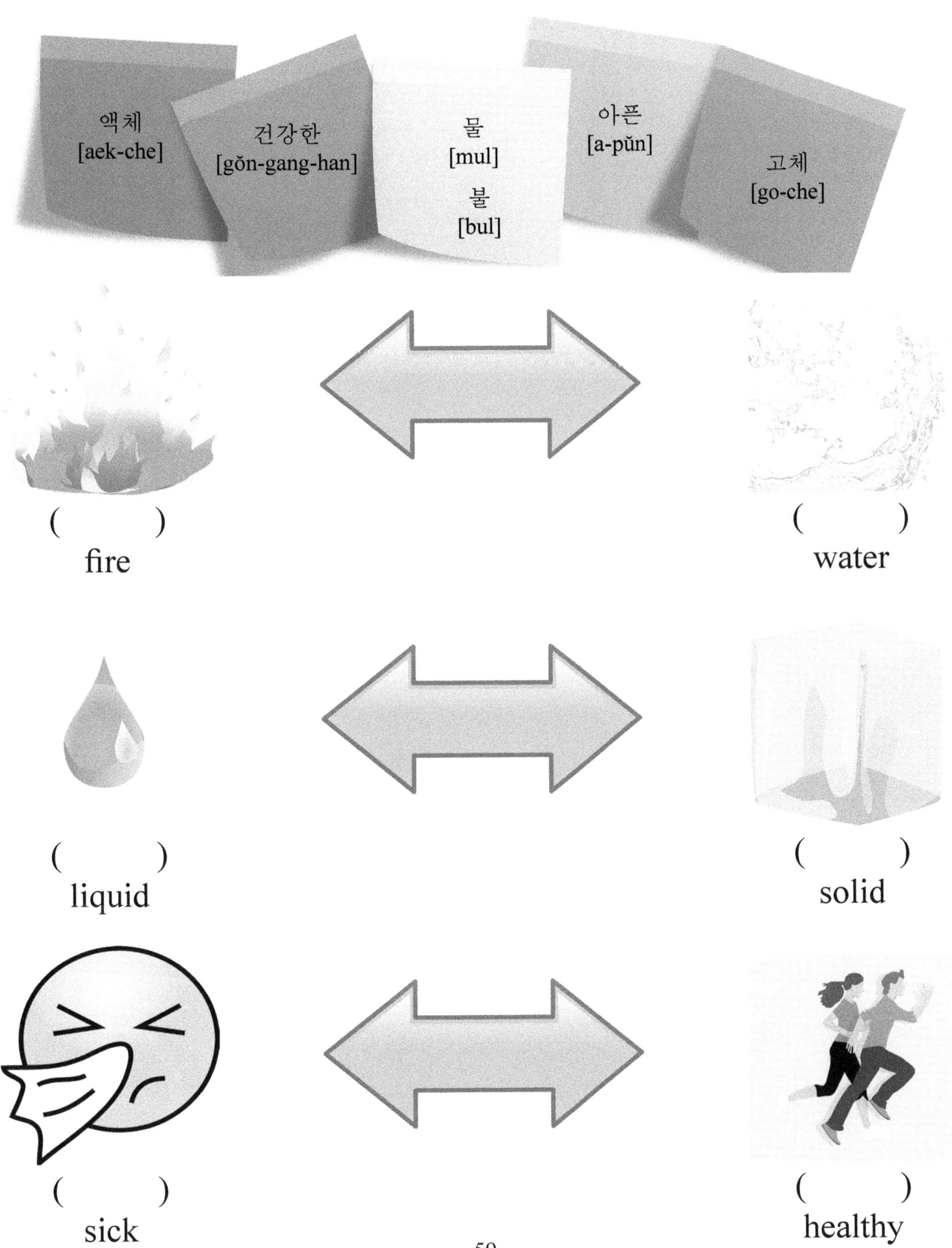
액체
[aek-che]
건강한
[gŏn-gang-han]
물
[mul]
불
[bul]
아픈
[a-pŭn]
고체
[go-che]
(　　)
fire
(　　)
water
(　　)
liquid
(　　)
solid
(　　)
sick
(　　)
healthy

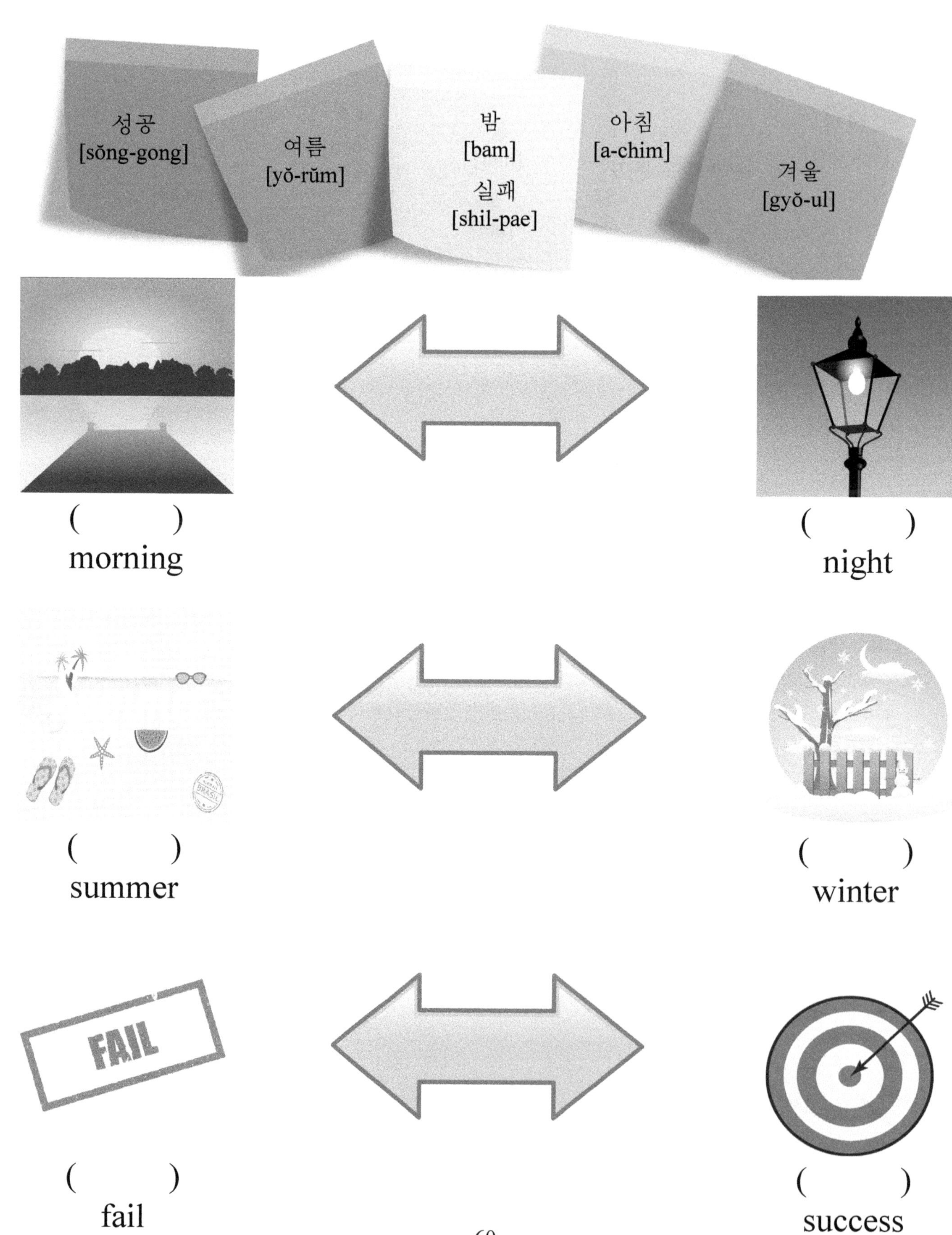

성공
[sŏng-gong]
여름
[yŏ-rŭm]
밤
[bam]
실패
[shil-pae]
아침
[a-chim]
겨울
[gyŏ-ul]
FAIL
( )
morning
( )
night
( )
summer
( )
winter
( )
fail
( )
success

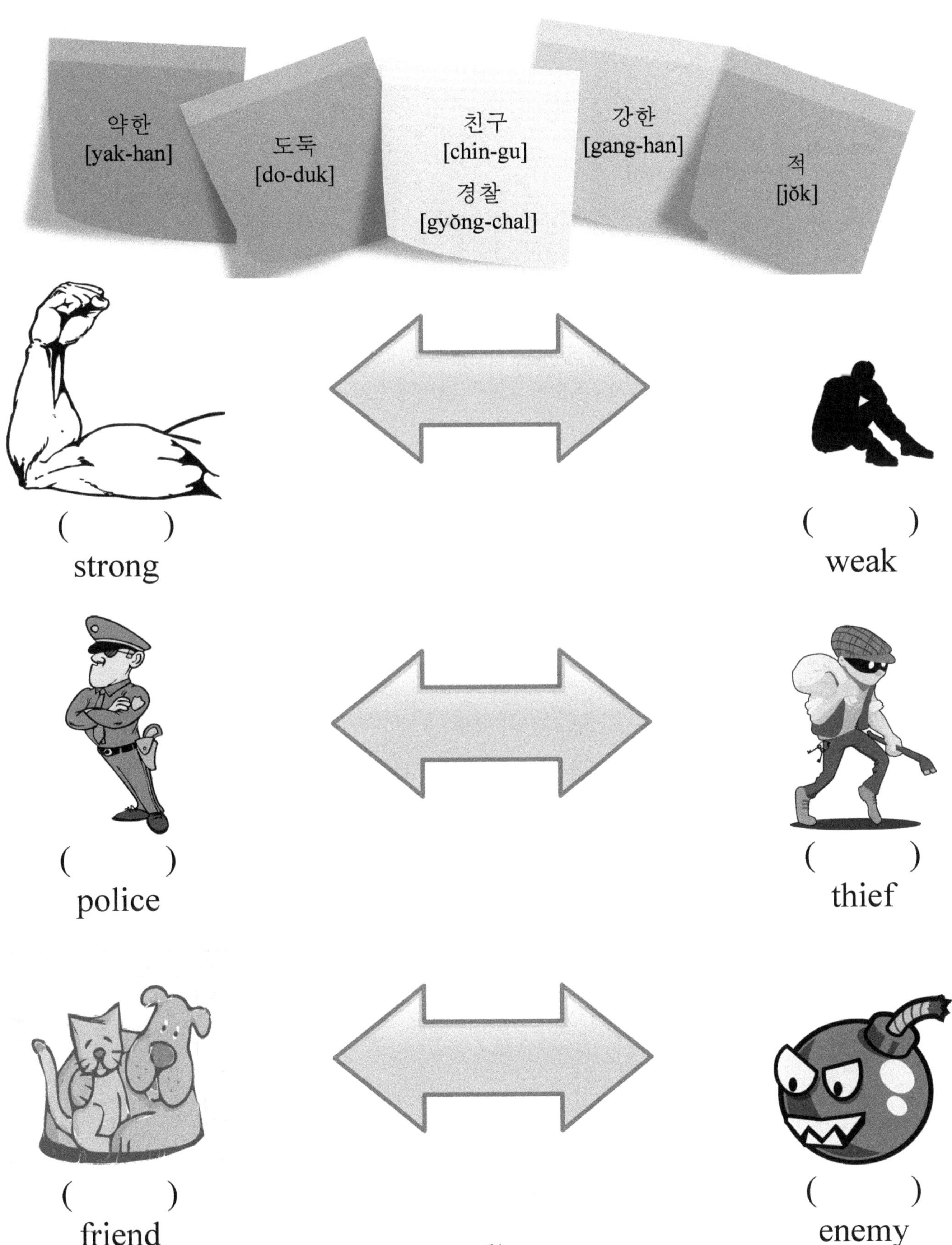
약한
[yak-han]
도둑
[do-duk]
친구
[chin-gu]
경찰
[gyŏng-chal]
강한
[gang-han]
적
[jŏk]
(   )
strong
(   )
weak
(   )
police
(   )
thief
(   )
friend
(   )
enemy

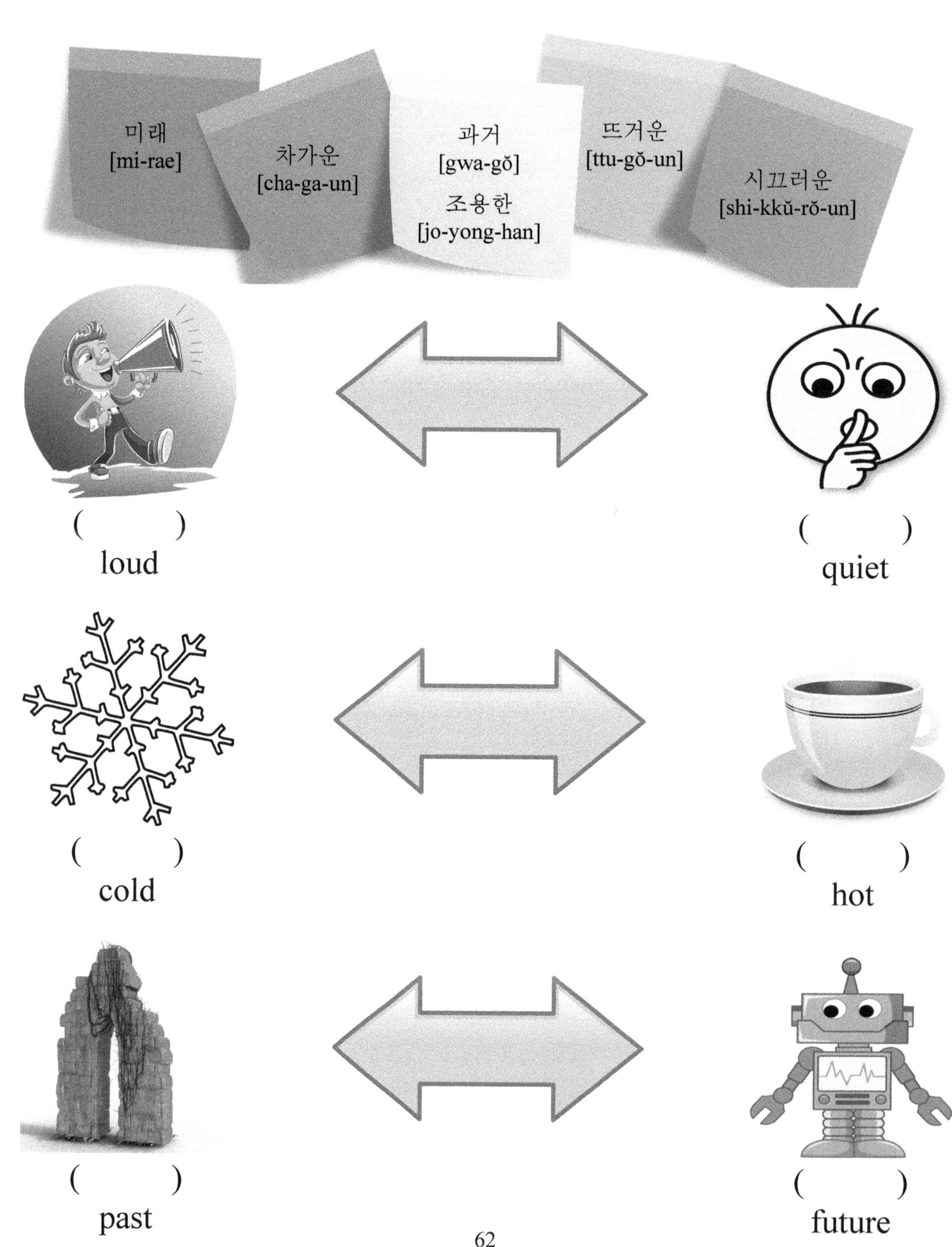
미래
[mi-rae]
차가운
[cha-ga-un]
과거
[gwa-gŏ]
조용한
[jo-yong-han]
뜨거운
[ttu-gŏ-un]
시끄러운
[shi-kkŭ-rŏ-un]
(   )
loud
(   )
quiet
(   )
cold
(   )
hot
(   )
past
(   )
future

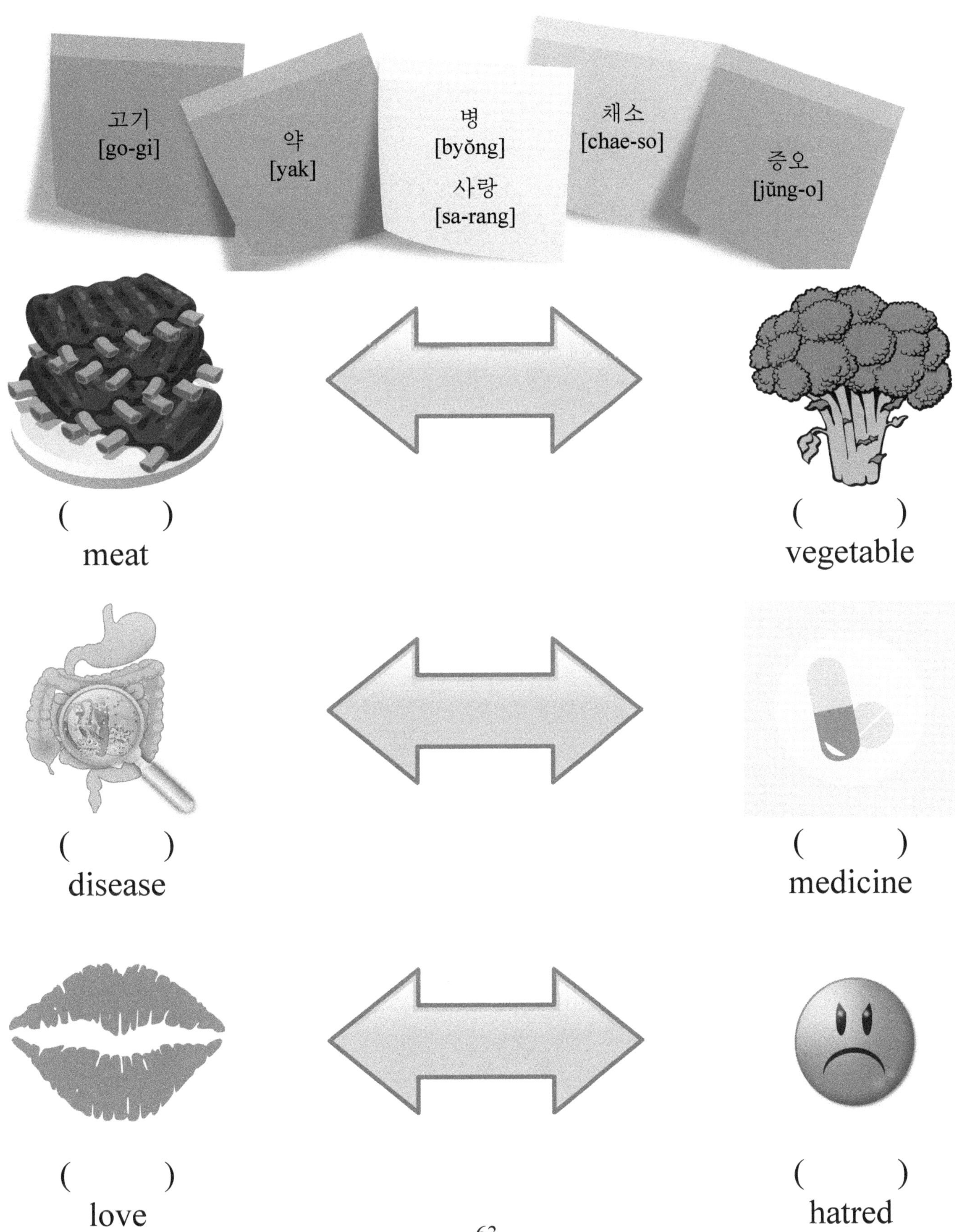
고기
[go-gi]
약
[yak]
병
[byŏng]
사랑
[sa-rang]
채소
[chae-so]
증오
[jŭng-o]
(   )
meat
(   )
vegetable
(   )
disease
(   )
medicine
(   )
love
(   )
hatred

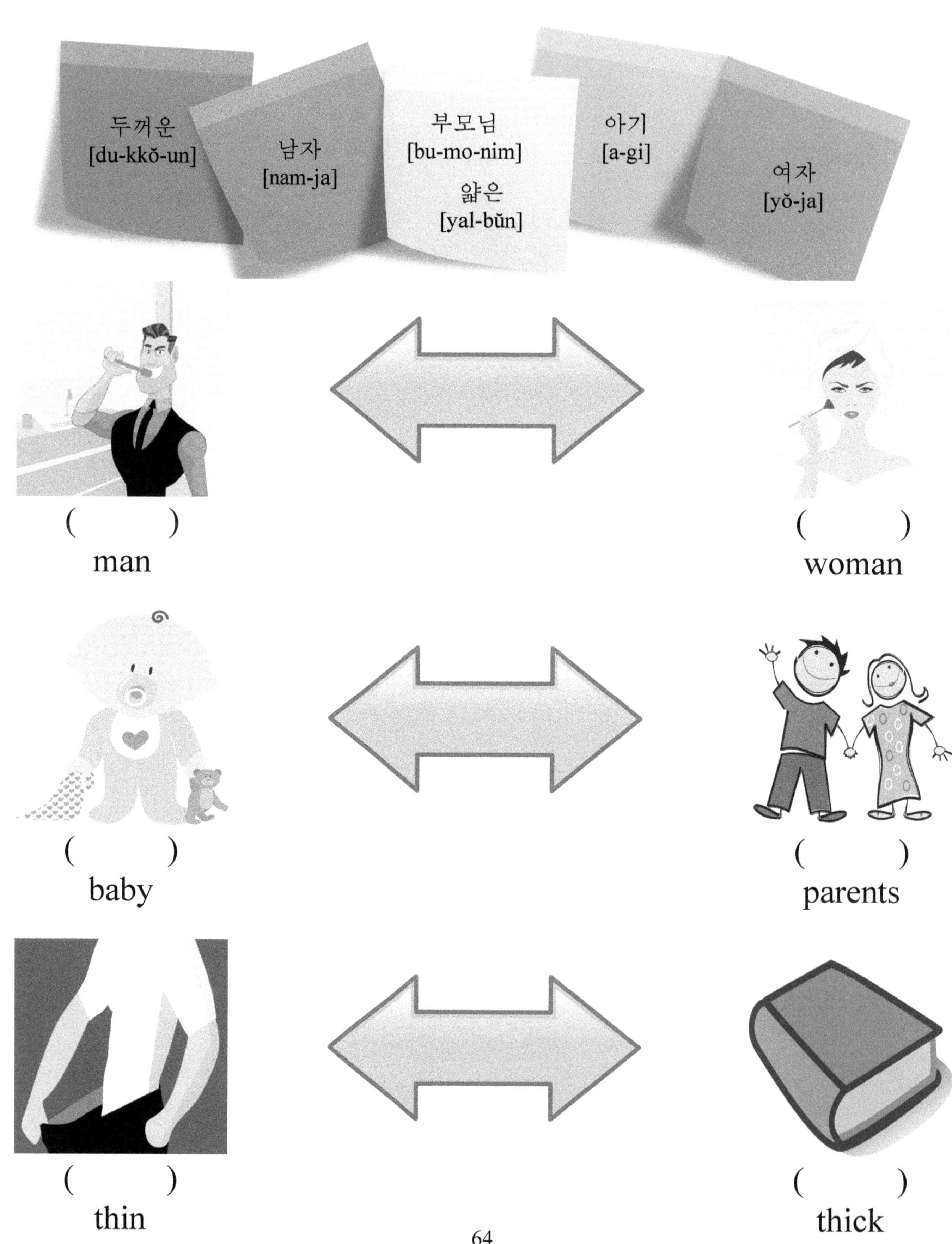
두꺼운
[du-kkŏ-un]
남자
[nam-ja]
부모님
[bu-mo-nim]
얇은
[yal-bŭn]
아기
[a-gi]
여자
[yŏ-ja]
(   )
man
(   )
woman
(   )
baby
(   )
parents
(   )
thin
(   )
thick

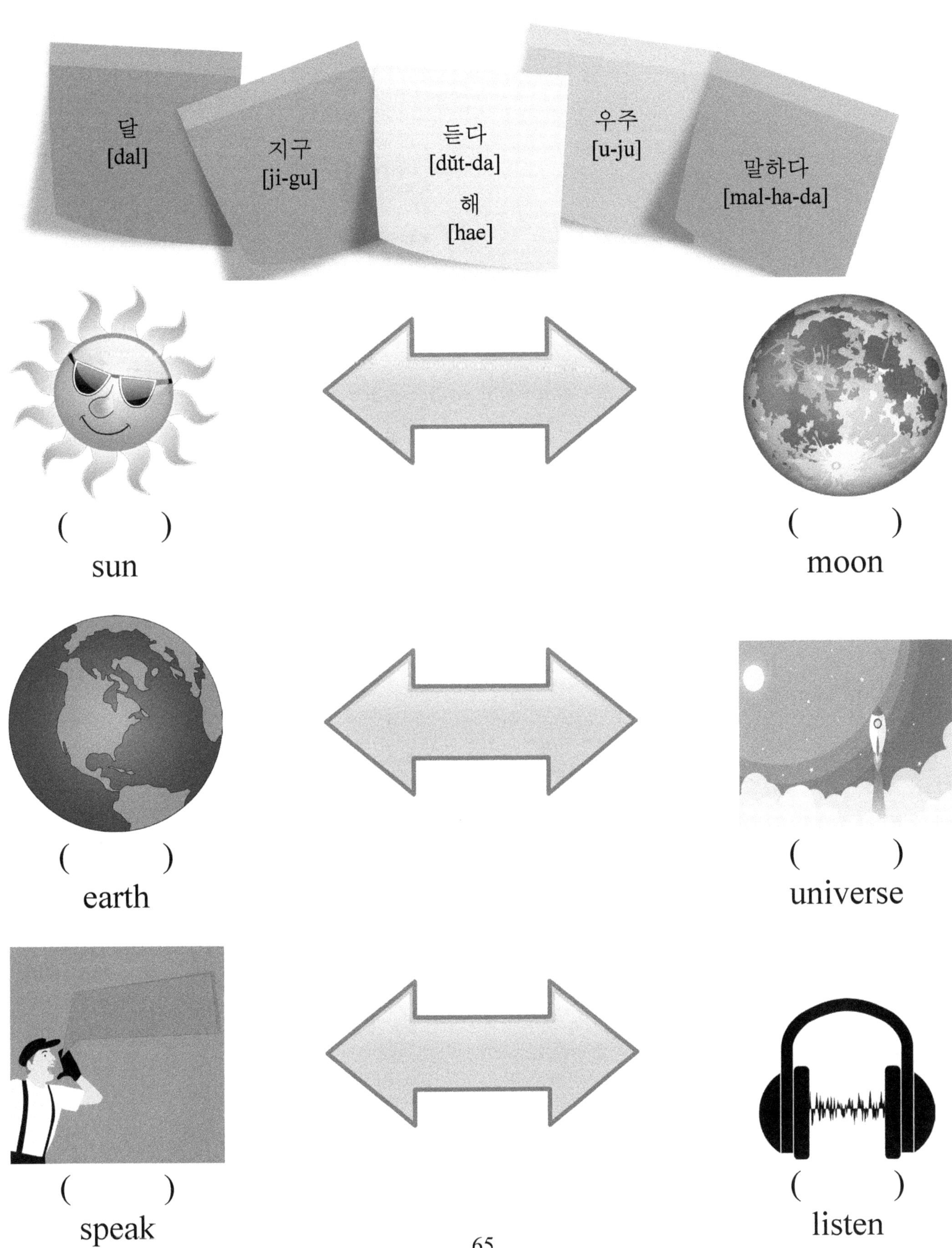
달
[dal]
지구
[ji-gu]
듣다
[dŭt-da]
해
[hae]
우주
[u-ju]
말하다
[mal-ha-da]
( )
sun
( )
moon
( )
earth
( )
universe
( )
speak
( )
listen

ANSWER KEY

(동물)
[dong-mul]
animal
(식물)
[shik-mul]
plant
(땅)
[ttang]
land
(하늘)
[ha-nul]
sky

(어두운)
[o-du-un]
dark
(밝은)
[bal-gŭn]
bright
(배고픈)
[bae-go-pŭn]
hungry
(배부른)
[bae-bu-rŭn]
full
(걷다)
[got-da]
walk
(뛰다)
[ttwi-da]
run

(느린)
[nŭ-rin]
slow
(빠른)
[bba-rŭn]
fast
(높은)
[no-pŭn]
high
(낮은)
[na-jun]
low
(어른)
[ŏ-rŭn]
adult
(어린이)
[ŏ-rin-i]
child

(천사)
[chŏn-sa]
angel
(악마)
[ak-ma]
devil
(늦은)
[nu-jŭn]
late
(이른)
[i-rŭn]
early
(승리)
[sŭng-ri]
victory
(패배)
[pae-bae]
loss

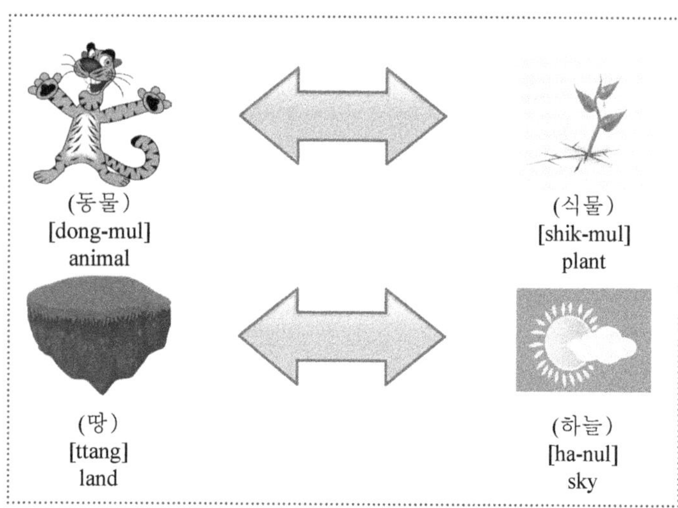

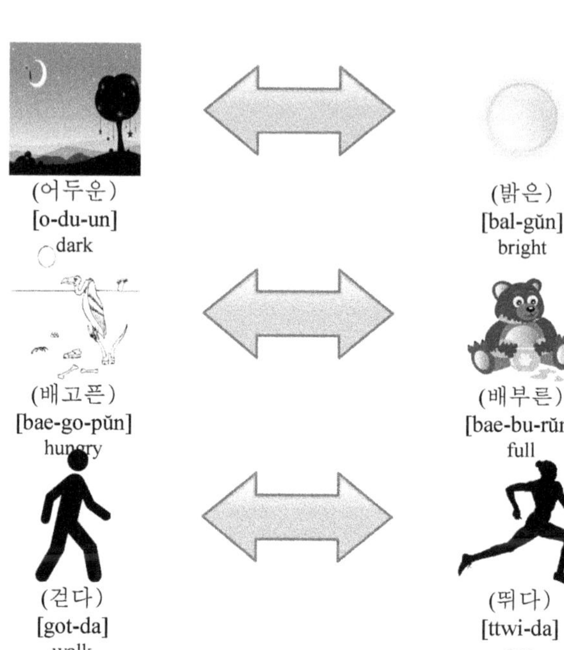

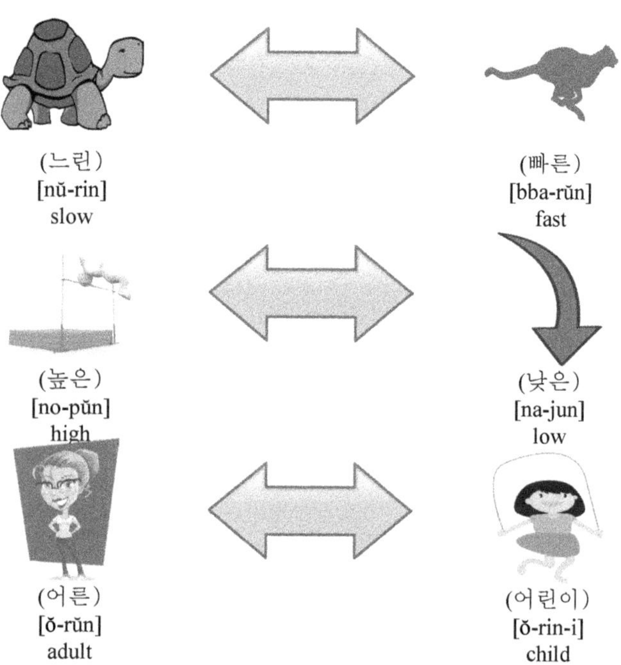

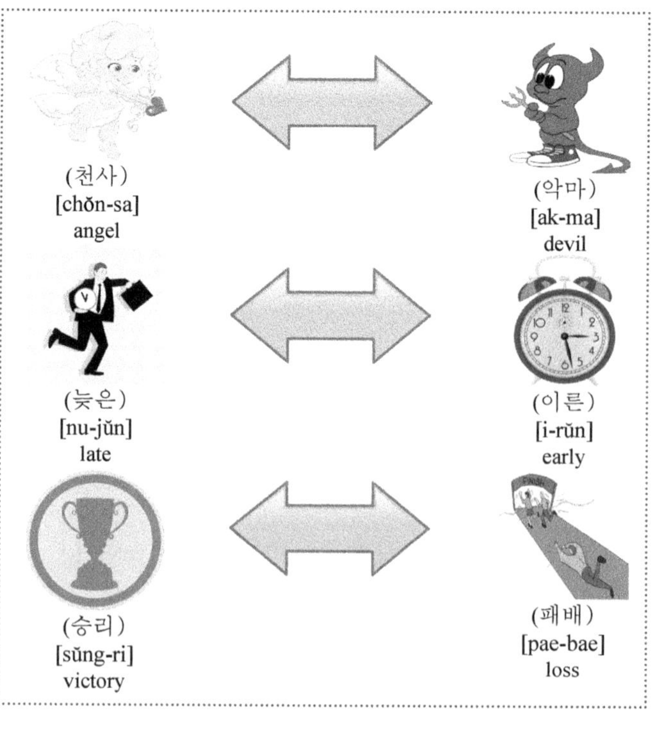

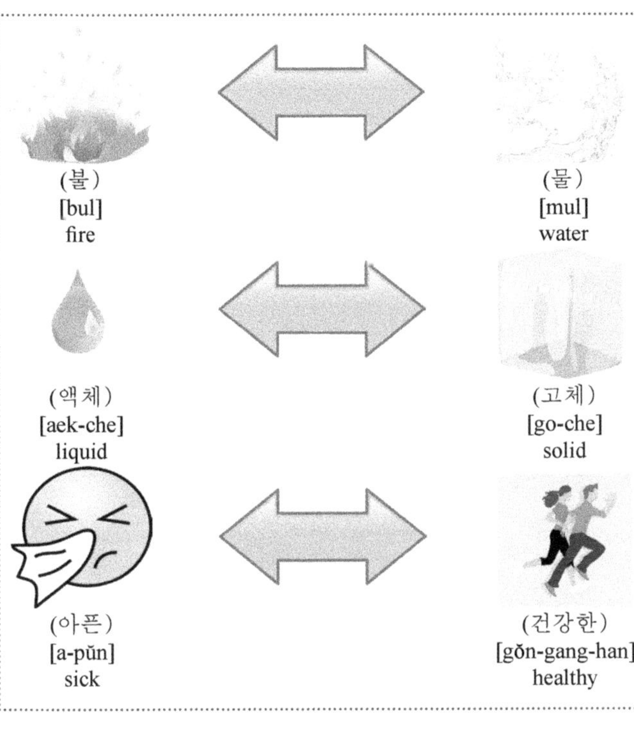
(불)
[bul]
fire
(물)
[mul]
water
(액체)
[aek-che]
liquid
(고체)
[go-che]
solid
(아픈)
[a-pŭn]
sick
(건강한)
[gŏn-gang-han]
healthy

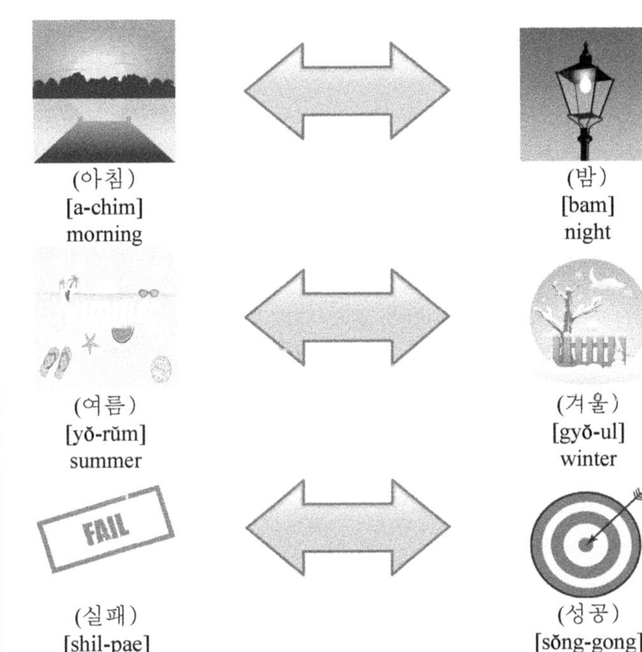
(아침)
[a-chim]
morning
(밤)
[bam]
night
(여름)
[yŏ-rŭm]
summer
(겨울)
[gyŏ-ul]
winter
FAIL
(실패)
[shil-pae]
fail
(성공)
[sŏng-gong]
success

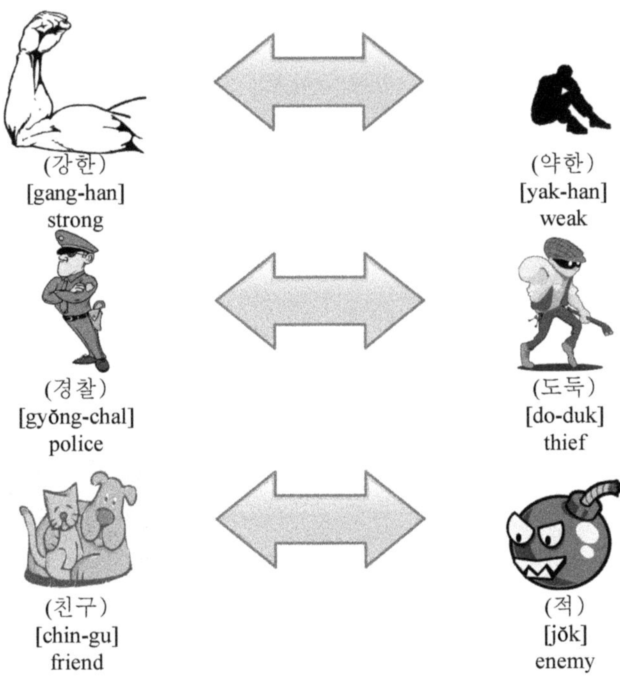
(강한)
[gang-han]
strong
(약한)
[yak-han]
weak
(경찰)
[gyŏng-chal]
police
(도둑)
[do-duk]
thief
(친구)
[chin-gu]
friend
(적)
[jŏk]
enemy

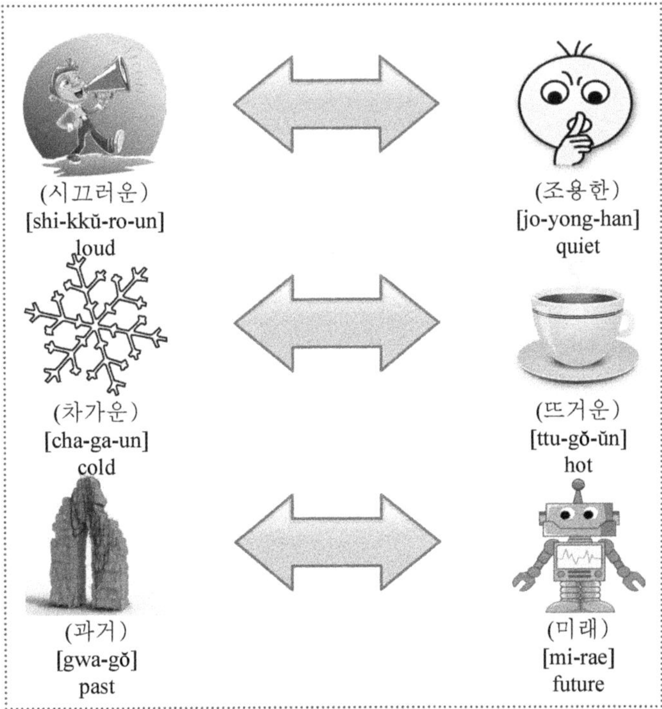
(시끄러운)
[shi-kkŭ-ro-un]
loud
(조용한)
[jo-yong-han]
quiet
(차가운)
[cha-ga-un]
cold
(뜨거운)
[ttu-gŏ-ŭn]
hot
(과거)
[gwa-gŏ]
past
(미래)
[mi-rae]
future

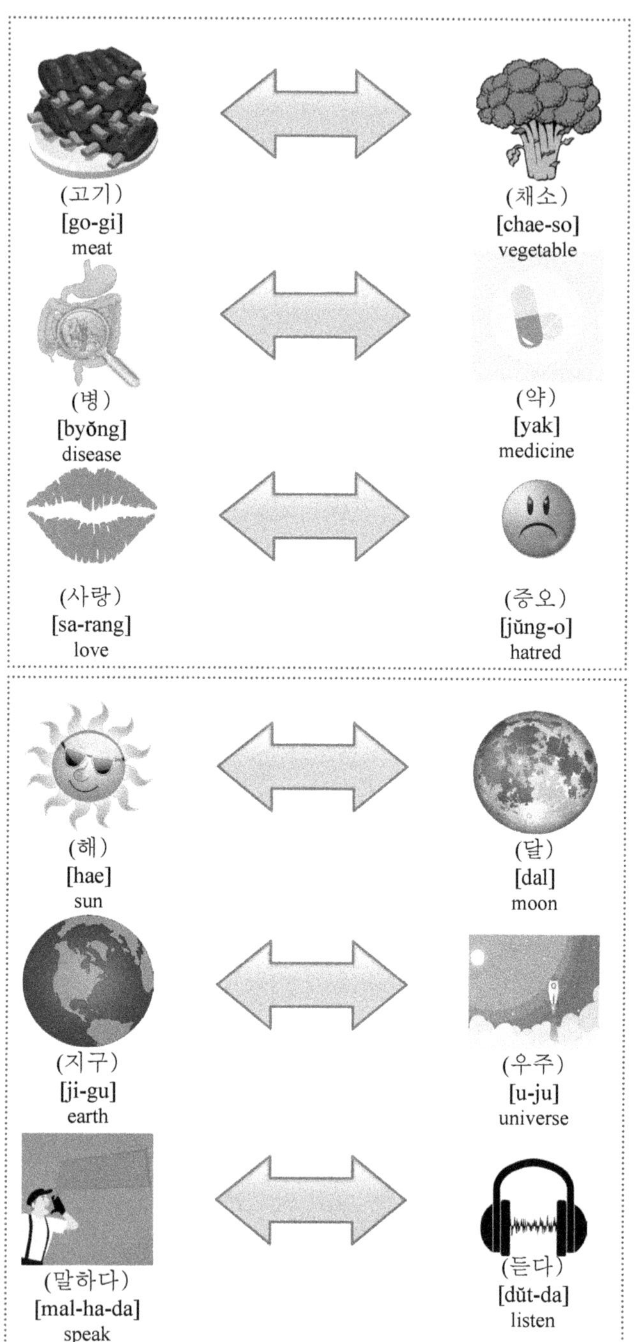

(고기)
[go-gi]
meat
(채소)
[chae-so]
vegetable
(병)
[byŏng]
disease
(약)
[yak]
medicine
(사랑)
[sa-rang]
love
(증오)
[jŭng-o]
hatred
(해)
[hae]
sun
(달)
[dal]
moon
(지구)
[ji-gu]
earth
(우주)
[u-ju]
universe
(말하다)
[mal-ha-da]
speak
(듣다)
[dŭt-da]
listen

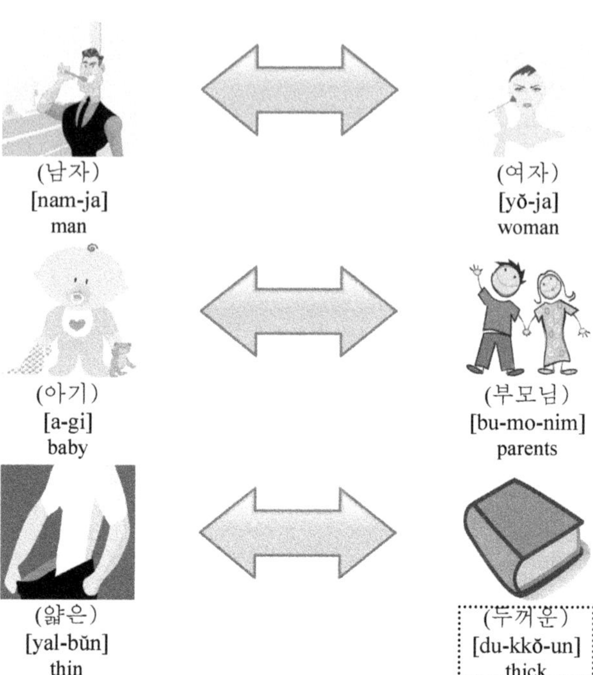

(남자)
[nam-ja]
man
(여자)
[yŏ-ja]
woman
(아기)
[a-gi]
baby
(부모님)
[bu-mo-nim]
parents
(얇은)
[yal-bŭn]
thin
(두꺼운)
[du-kkŏ-un]
thick

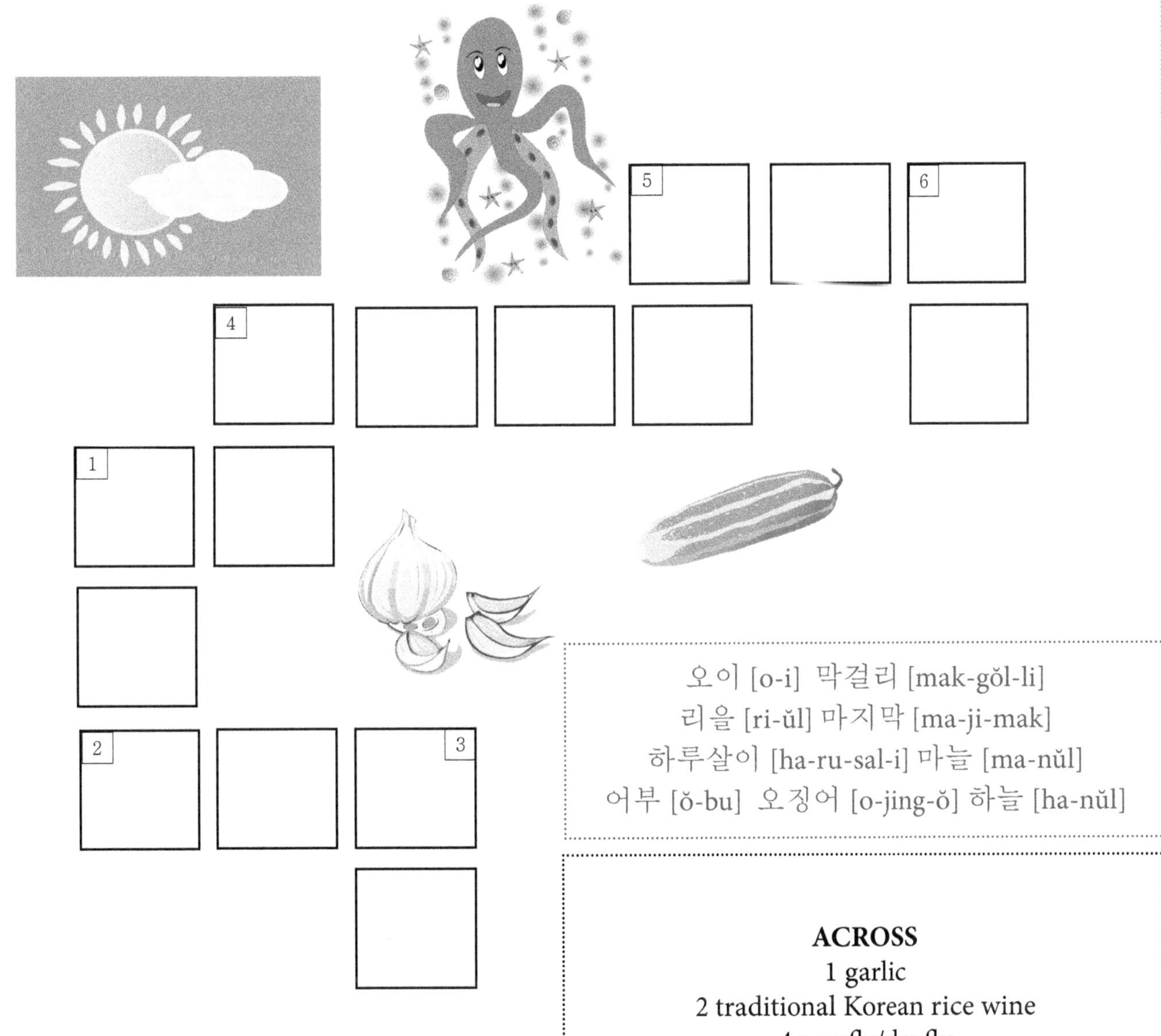

오이 [o-i] 막걸리 [mak-gŏl-li]
리을 [ri-ŭl] 마지막 [ma-ji-mak]
하루살이 [ha-ru-sal-i] 마늘 [ma-nŭl]
어부 [ŏ-bu] 오징어 [o-jing-ŏ] 하늘 [ha-nŭl]

ACROSS
1 garlic
2 traditional Korean rice wine
4 mayfly/dayfly
5 squid/cuttlefish

DOWN
1 last, final
3 Korean consonant ㄹ
4 sky
6 Fisherman

수박 [su-bak] 자존심 [ja-jon-shim]
허수아비 [hŏ-su-a-bi] 심장 [shim-jang]
소비자 [so-bi-ja] 소독 [so-dok]

ACROSS
1 scarecrow
2 traditional Korean rice wine
3 sanitization
4 pride

DOWN
2 watermelon
3 consumer
5 heart

1

6

5

2

4

3

서울 [sŏ-ul] 가르마 [ga-rŭ-ma]
구름 [gu-rŭm] 여분 [yŏ-bun]
참기름 [cham-gi-rŭm] 겨울 [gyŏ-ul]
가을 [ga-ŭl] 구분 [gu-bun]
여자친구 [yŏ-ja-chin-gu] 참새 [cham-sae]

ACROSS
1 sparrow
2 cloud
3 extra/excess/surplus
4 fall/autumn
5 winter

DOWN
1 sesame oil
2 division/classification
3 girlfriend
5 parting (of hair)
6 capital of Korea

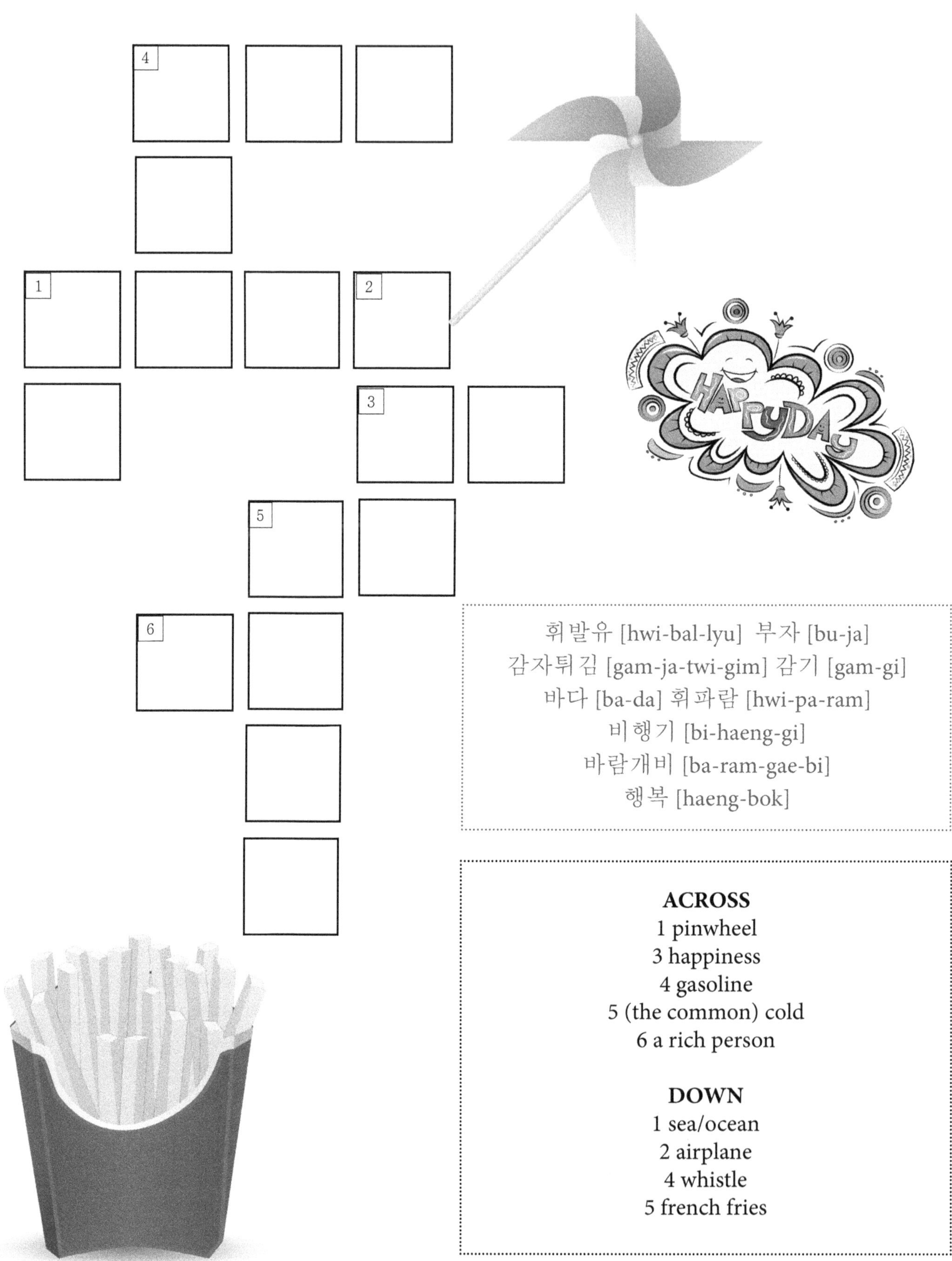

휘발유 [hwi-bal-lyu] 부자 [bu-ja]
감자튀김 [gam-ja-twi-gim] 감기 [gam-gi]
바다 [ba-da] 휘파람 [hwi-pa-ram]
비행기 [bi-haeng-gi]
바람개비 [ba-ram-gae-bi]
행복 [haeng-bok]

ACROSS
1 pinwheel
3 happiness
4 gasoline
5 (the common) cold
6 a rich person

DOWN
1 sea/ocean
2 airplane
4 whistle
5 french fries

ANSWER KEY

5 오 징 6 어
4 하 루 살 이 부
1 마 늘
지
2 막 걸 3 리
을

3 소 독
1 허 2 수 아 비
박 4 자 존 5 심
장

1 참 새 6 서
기 5 겨 울
2 구 름 4 가 을
3 여 분 르
자 마
친
구

4 휘 발 유
파
1 바 람 개 2 비
다 3 행 복
5 감 기
6 부 자
튀
김

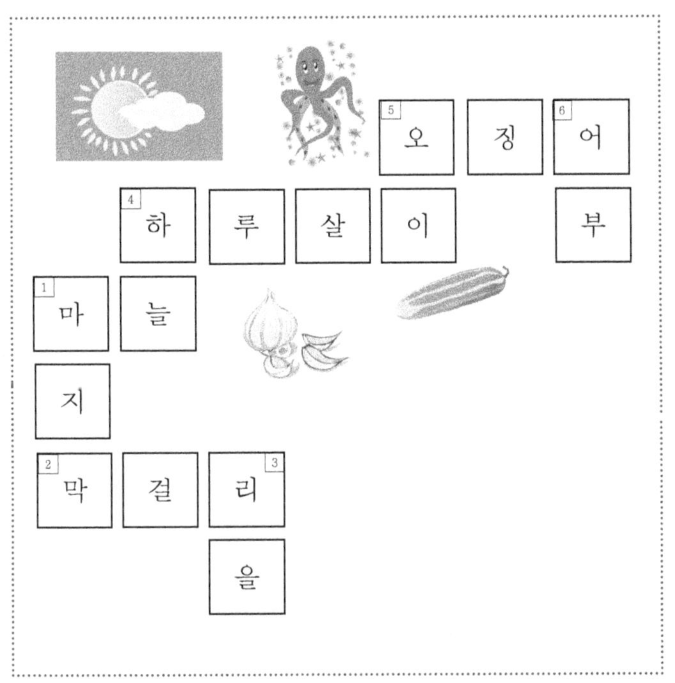

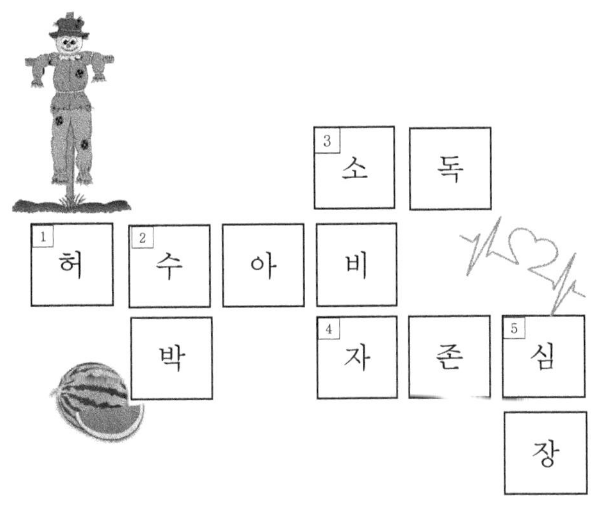

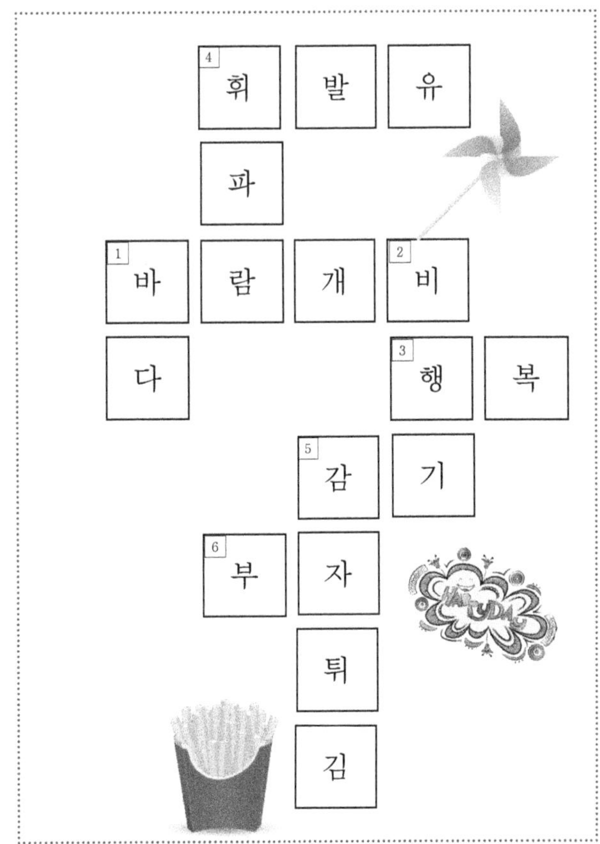

MULTIPLE QUESTIONS

Use a check mark ✔ to select the word that matchest the description.

1	dentist's office	◯ 사과 [sa-gwa] ◯ 백화점 [baek-hwa-jŏm]	◯ 치과 [chi-gwa] ◯ 학원 [hak-won]
2	eraser	◯ 연필 [yŏn-pil] ◯ 지우개 [ji-u-gae]	◯ 공책 [gong-chaek] ◯ 분필 [bun-pil]
3	green tea	◯ 홍차 [hong-cha] ◯ 맥주 [maek-ju]	◯ 모과차 [mo-gwa-cha] ◯ 녹차 [nok-cha]
4	audience	◯ 관중 [gwan-jung] ◯ 학생 [hak-saeng]	◯ 이모 [i-mo] ◯ 사장님 [sa-jang-nim]
5	duck	◯ 오리 [o-ri] ◯ 요리 [yo-ri]	◯ 고리 [go-ri] ◯ 도리 [do-ri]
6	torture	◯ 대문 [dae-mun] ◯ 이야기 [i-ya-gi]	◯ 고문 [go-mun] ◯ 소문 [so-mun]
7	(eye) glasses	◯ 모자 [mo-ja] ◯ 수건 [su-gŏn]	◯ 안과 [an-gwa] ◯ 안경 [an-gyŏng]
8	window	◯ 벽 [byŏk] ◯ 집 [jip]	◯ 창문 [chang-mun] ◯ 바닥 [ba-dak]

9	acknowledgement/recognition	꿈 [kkum]	인정 [in-jŏng]	수정 [su-jŏng]	인기 [in-gi]
10	education	교포 [gyo-po]	학생 [hak-saeng]	교육 [gyo-yuk]	교사 [gyo-sa]
11	seagull	갈매기 [gal-mae-gi]	매 [mae]	독수리 [dok-su-ri]	기러기 [gi-rŏ-gi]
12	letter/mail	수필 [su-pil]	잡지 [jap-ji]	시험 [shi-hŏm]	편지 [pyŏn-ji]
13	applause	박수 [bak-su]	박 [bak]	수박 [su-bak]	호박 [ho-bak]
14	rose	장미 [jang-mi]	식물 [shik-mul]	꽃 [kkot]	채소 [chae-so]
15	earthquake	지구 [ji-gu]	지진 [ji-jin]	바위 [ba-wi]	파괴 [pa-goe]
16	maze	미행 [mi-haeng]	지도 [ji-do]	미로 [mi-ro]	기로 [gi-ro]
17	newspaper	신호 [shin-ho]	신문 [shin-mun]	소식 [so-sik]	소문 [so-mun]
18	balloon	바람 [ba-ram]	바람개비 [ba-ram-gae-bi]	풍차 [pung-cha]	풍선 [pung-sŏn]

No.	Word	Option 1	Option 2	Option 3	Option 4
19	bean	콩 [kong]	돈 [don]	치과 [cotton]	솜 [som]
20	wound/cut	치마 [chi-ma]	상처 [sang-chŏ]	배낭 [bae-nang]	가방 [ga-bang]
21	spoon	숟가락 [sut-ga-rak]	개미 [gae-mi]	바지 [ba-ji]	노래 [no-rae]
22	ladder	배구 [bae-gu]	사다리 [sa-da-ri]	친구 [chin-gu]	세로 [se-ro]
23	movie	영원 [yŏng-wŏn]	영하 [yŏng-ha]	영화 [yŏng-hwa]	영상 [yŏng-sang]
24	soccer	축사 [chuk-sa]	축하 [chuk-ha]	축구 [chuk-gu]	축가 [chuk-ga]
25	marriage	신혼 [shin-hon]	결혼 [gyŏl-hon]	신비 [shin-bi]	결국 [gyŏl-guk]
26	swimming pool	수난 [su-nan]	수질 [su-jil]	수영장 [su-yŏng-jang]	수비 [su-bi]
27	reservation	예약 [ye-yak]	예리 [ye-ri]	예금 [ye-gŭm]	예고 [ye-go]
28	chopsticks	발가락 [bal-ga-rak]	젓가락 [jŏt-ga-rak]	숫가락 [sut-ga-rak]	수술 [su-sul]

29 public transportation

- ○ 대한민국 [dae-han-min-guk]
- ○ 대중교통 [dae-jung-gyo-tong]
- ○ 대로 [dae-ro]
- ○ 대종상 [dae-jong-sang]

30 mistake

- ○ 실패 [shil-pae]
- ○ 실책 [shil-chaek]
- ○ 실수 [shil-su]
- ○ 실리 [shil-li]

31 misunderstanding

- ○ 오해 [o-hae]
- ○ 오류 [o-ryu]
- ○ 치과 [chi-gwa]
- ○ 치과 [chi-gwa]

32 conversation

- ○ 대표 [dae-pyo]
- ○ 대안 [dae-an]
- ○ 대리 [dae-ri]
- ○ 대화 [dae-hwa]

33 pronunciation

- ○ 발음 [bal-ŭm]
- ○ 벼름 [byŏ-rŭm]
- ○ 바람 [ba-ram]
- ○ 버릇 [bŏ-rŭt]

34 pencil

- ○ 연필 [yŏn-pil]
- ○ 연습 [yŏn-sŭp]
- ○ 예복 [ye-bok]
- ○ 예습 [ye-sŭp]

35 paper

- ○ 장인 [jang-in]
- ○ 종이 [jong-i]
- ○ 지연 [ji-yŏn]
- ○ 종 [jong]

36 tree

- ○ 내용 [nae-yong]
- ○ 녹말 [nok-mal]
- ○ 나무 [na-mu]
- ○ 치과 [chi-gwa]

37 mountain

- ○ 신 [shin]
- ○ 산 [san]
- ○ 상 [sang]
- ○ 손 [son]

38 wind

- ○ 보람 [bo-ram]
- ○ 벼랑 [byŏ-rang]
- ○ 바름 [ba-rŭm]
- ○ 바람 [ba-ram]

39	mushroom	변신 [byŏn-shin]	버섯 [bŏ-sŏt]
		변심 [byŏn-shim]	부산 [bu-san]
40	needle	비누 [bi-nu]	비늘 [bi-nŭl]
		바늘 [ba-nŭl]	나비 [na-bi]
41	notebook	공책 [gong-chaek]	혜택 [hye-taek]
		책임 [chaek-im]	이해 [i-hae]
42	professor	교회 [gyo-hoe]	치수 [chi-su]
		기회 [gi-hoe]	교수 [gyo-su]
43	doll	인형 [in-hyŏng]	형제 [hyŏng-je]
		안경 [an-gyŏng]	풍경 [pung-gyŏng]
44	department store	백화점 [baek-hwa-jŏm]	무지개 [mu-ji-gae]
		배추 [bae-chu]	김장 [gim-jang]
45	crystal	소장 [so-jang]	수정 [su-jŏng]
		수장 [su-jang]	소정 [so-jŏng]
46	question	시험 [shi-hŏm]	향수 [hyang-su]
		질문 [jil-mun]	해답 [hae-dap]
47	cell phone	자전거 [ja-jŏn-gŏ]	휴대폰 [hyu-dae-pon]
		침대 [chim-dae]	지갑 [ji-gap]
48	post office	백화점 [baek-hwa-jŏm]	경찰서 [gyŏng-chal-sŏ]
		상점 [sang-jŏm]	우체국 [u-che-guk]

49	homework	○ 성과 [sŏng-gwa]	○ 생가 [saeng-ga]
		○ 숙제 [suk-je]	○ 성인 [sŏng-in]
50	pants	○ 배영 [bae-yŏng]	○ 바람 [ba-ram]
		○ 반사 [ban-sa]	○ 바지 [ba-ji]
51	clock	○ 시간 [shi-gan]	○ 시차 [shi-cha]
		○ 시계 [shi-gye]	○ 시야 [shi-ya]
52	skirt	○ 치과 [chi-gwa]	○ 하마 [ha-ma]
		○ 목도리 [mok-do-ri]	○ 치마 [chi-ma]
53	toy	○ 운동장 [un-dong-jang]	○ 장남감 [jang-jan-gam]
		○ 도구 [do-gu]	○ 악기 [ak-gi]
54	chair	○ 액자 [aek-ja]	○ 패자 [pae-ja]
		○ 의자 [ŭi-ja]	○ 책상 [chaek-sang]
55	underwear	○ 잠옷 [jam-ot]	○ 겉옷 [gŏt-ot]
		○ 옷장 [ot-jang]	○ 속옷 [sok-ot]
56	handshake	○ 박수 [bak-su]	○ 세수 [se-su]
		○ 치수 [chi-su]	○ 악수 [ak-su]
57	rainbow	○ 찌개 [chi-gae]	○ 태풍 [tae-pung]
		○ 무지개 [mu-ji-gae]	○ 태양 [tae-yang]
58	shadow	○ 기름 [gi-rŭm]	○ 구름 [gu-rŭm]
		○ 거름 [gŏ-rŭm]	○ 그림자 [gŭ-rim-ja]

59	wrong answer	답신 [dap-shin]	오답 [o-dap]
		문답 [mun-dap]	정답 [jŏng-dap]
60	favor	부부 [bu-bu]	부탁 [bu-tak]
		반사 [ban-sa]	배신 [bae-shin]
61	electricity	종류 [jong-ryu]	전기 [jŏn-gi]
		장기 [jang-gi]	전사 [jŏn-sa]
62	waste	기러기 [gi-rŏ-gi]	그림 [gŭ-rim]
		쓰레기 [ssŭ-re-gi]	가르기 [ga-rŭ-gi]
63	dictionary	수전 [su-jŏn]	시전 [shi-jŏn]
		생전 [saeng-jŏn]	사전 [sa-jŏn]
64	religion	종교 [jong-gyo]	정기 [jŏng-gi]
		장가 [jang-ga]	종기 [jong-gi]
65	envelope	봉투 [bong-tu]	방지 [bang-ji]
		봉지 [bong-ji]	빙자 [bing-ja]
66	salt	양념 [yang-nyŏm]	소금 [so-gŭm]
		반찬 [ban-chan]	휴지 [hyu-ji]
67	sugar	식초 [shik-cho]	후추 [hu-chu]
		설탕 [gŏn-gang]	배추 [bae-chu]
68	soy sauce	긴장 [gin-jang]	김장 [gim-jang]
		간장 [gan-jang]	건강 [gŏn-gang]

69	country/nation	나라 [na-ra]	누리 [nu-ri]
		노래 [no-rae]	내리 [nae-ri]
70	cleaning (a room)	채소 [chae-so]	청소 [chŏng-so]
		친구 [chin-gu]	칭송 [ching-song]
71	memory	기억 [gi-ŏk]	기록 [gi-rok]
		기념 [gi-nyŏm]	기밀 [gi-mil]
72	season	치과 [chi-gwa]	치과 [chi-gwa]
		치과 [chi-gwa]	치과 [chi-gwa]
73	machine	지게 [ji-ge]	비계 [bi-gye]
		기계 [gi-gye]	세계 [se-gye]
74	refrigerator	창문 [chang-mun]	부엌 [bu-ŏk]
		냉장고 [naeng-jang-go]	거실 [gŏ-shil]
75	correct answer	답신 [dap-shin]	정답 [jŏng-dap]
		답례 [dap-rye]	답보 [dap-bo]
76	car	마루 [ma-ru]	자동차 [ja-dong-cha]
		치과 [chi-gwa]	바퀴 [ba-kwi]
77	river	강 [gang]	가위 [ga-wi]
		개인 [gae-in]	길 [gil]
78	trip	이행 [i-haeng]	여행 [yŏ-haeng]
		야행 [ya-haeng]	요행 [yo-haeng]

No.	Word	Option 1	Option 2	Option 3	Option 4
79	number	수술 [su-sul]	숫자 [sut-ja]	기록 [gi-rok]	가루 [ga-ru]
80	dining table	식기 [shik-gi]	식사 [shik-sa]	식료 [shik-ryo]	식탁 [shik-tak]
81	button	당근 [dang-gŭm]	단추 [dan-chu]	호박 [ho-bak]	한밤 [han-bam]
82	money	솜 [som]	몸 [mom]	곰 [gom]	돈 [don]
83	glove	장갑 [chi-gwa]	고무 [go-mu]	선동 [sŏn-dong]	양복 [yang-bok]
84	shoe(s)	신장 [shin-jang]	심장 [shim-jang]	신발 [shin-bal]	가발 [ga-bal]
85	desk	책장 [chaek-jang]	책가방 [chaek-ga-bang]	체면 [che-myŏn]	책상 [chaek-sang]
86	screen	화면 [hwa-myŏn]	가면 [ga-myŏn]	초면 [cho-myŏn]	대면 [dae-myŏn]
87	advertisement	개인 [gae-in]	광고 [gwang-go]	관광 [gwan-gwang]	기강 [gi-gang]
88	breaking news	설명 [sŏl-myŏng]	화질 [hwa-jil]	전보 [jŏn-bo]	속보 [sok-bo]

89	recommendation	추천 [chu-chŏn]	초대 [cho-dae]	체조 [che-jo]	체육 [che-yuk]
90	mirror	가을 [ga-ŭl]	거울 [gŏ-ul]	기울기 [gi-ul-gi]	개울 [gae-ul]
91	rumor	소라 [so-ra]	소개 [so-gae]	소주 [so-ju]	소문 [so-mun]
92	airport	역 [yŏk]	공항 [gong-hang]	바닥 [ba-dak]	정류장 [jŏng-ryu-jang]
93	history	예의 [ye-ŭi]	병원 [byŏng-wŏn]	비밀 [bi-mil]	역사 [yŏk-sa]
94	future	지금 [ji-gŭm]	태도 [tae-do]	미래 [mi-rae]	미술 [mi-sul]
95	past	내일 [nae-il]	과거 [gwa-gŏ]	어제 [ŏ-je]	미래 [mi-rae]
96	expectation	기침 [gi-chim]	후회 [hu-hoe]	바로 [ba-ro]	기대 [gi-dae]
97	reality	예고 [ye-go]	현실 [hyŏn-sil]	배분 [bae-bun]	치맥 [chi-maek]
98	accolade/compliment	하나 [ha-na]	해방 [hae-bang]	칭찬 [ching-chan]	마무리 [ma-mu-ri]

ANSWER KEY

1	dentist's office	사과 [sa-gwa]	✔ 치과 [chi-gwa]	백화점 [baek-hwa-jŏm]	학원 [hak-won]
2	eraser	연필 [yŏn-pil]	공책 [gong-chaek]	✔ 지우개 [ji-u-gae]	분필 [bun-pil]
3	green tea	홍차 [hong-cha]	모과차 [mo-gwa-cha]	맥주 [maek-ju]	✔ 녹차 [nok-cha]
4	audience	✔ 관중 [gwan-jung]	이모 [i-mo]	학생 [hak-saeng]	사장님 [sa-jang-nim]
5	duck	✔ 오리 [o-ri]	고리 [go-ri]	요리 [yo-ri]	도리 [do-ri]
6	torture	대문 [dae-mun]	✔ 고문 [go-mun]	이야기 [i-ya-gi]	소문 [so-mun]
7	(eye) glasses	모자 [mo-ja]	안과 [an-gwa]	수건 [su-gŏn]	✔ 안경 [an-gyŏng]
8	window	벽 [byŏk]	✔ 창문 [chang-mun]	집 [jip]	바닥 [ba-dak]
9	acknowledgement/recognition	꿈 [kkum]	✔ 인정 [in-jŏng]	수정 [su-jŏng]	인기 [in-gi]
10	education	교포 [gyo-po]	학생 [hak-saeng]	✔ 교육 [gyo-yuk]	교사 [gyo-sa]
11	seagull	✔ 갈매기 [gal-mae-gi]	매 [mae]	독수리 [dok-su-ri]	기러기 [gi-rŏ-gi]
12	letter/mail	수필 [su-pil]	잡지 [jap-ji]	시험 [shi-hŏm]	✔ 편지 [pyŏn-ji]
13	applause	✔ 박수 [bak-su]	박 [bak]	수박 [su-bak]	호박 [ho-bak]
14	rose	✔ 장미 [jang-mi]	식물 [shik-mul]	꽃 [kkot]	채소 [chae-so]
15	earthquake	지구 [ji-gu]	✔ 지진 [ji-jin]	바위 [ba-wi]	파괴 [pa-goe]
16	maze	미행 [mi-haeng]	지도 [ji-do]	✔ 미로 [mi-ro]	기로 [gi-ro]
17	newspaper	신호 [shin-ho]	✔ 신문 [shin-mun]	소식 [so-sik]	소문 [so-mun]
18	balloon	바람 [ba-ram]	바람개비 [ba-ram-gae-bi]	풍차 [pung-cha]	✔ 풍선 [pung-sŏn]
19	bean	✔ 콩 [kong]	돈 [don]	치과 [cotton]	솜 [som]
20	wound/cut	치마 [chi-ma]	✔ 상처 [sang-chŏ]	배낭 [bae-nang]	가방 [ga-bang]
21	spoon	✔ 숟가락 [sut-ga-rak]	개미 [gae-mi]	바지 [ba-ji]	노래 [no-rae]
22	ladder	배구 [bae-gu]	✔ 사다리 [sa-da-ri]	친구 [chin-gu]	세로 [se-ro]
23	movie	영원 [yŏng-wŏn]	영하 [yŏng-ha]	✔ 영화 [yŏng-hwa]	영상 [yŏng-sang]
24	soccer	축사 [chuk-sa]	축하 [chuk-ha]	✔ 축구 [chuk-gu]	축가 [chuk-ga]
25	marriage	신혼 [shin-hon]	✔ 결혼 [gyŏl-hon]	신비 [shin-bi]	결국 [gyŏl-guk]
26	swimming pool	수난 [su-nan]	수질 [su-jil]	✔ 수영장 [su-yŏng-jang]	수비 [su-bi]
27	reservation	✔ 예약 [ye-yak]	예리 [ye-ri]	예금 [ye-gŭm]	예고 [ye-go]
28	chopsticks	발가락 [bal-ga-rak]	✔ 젓가락 [jŏt-ga-rak]	숫가락 [sut-ga-rak]	수술 [su-sul]
29	public transportation	대한민국 [dae-han-min-guk]	✔ 대중교통 [dae-jung-gyo-tong]	대로 [dae-ro]	대종상 [dae-jong-sang]
30	mistake	실패 [shil-pae]	실책 [shil-chaek]	✔ 실수 [shil-su]	실리 [shil-li]
31	misunderstanding	✔ 오해 [o-hae]	오류 [o-ryu]	치과 [chi-gwa]	치과 [chi-gwa]
32	conversation	대표 [dae-pyo]	대안 [dae-an]	대리 [dae-ri]	✔ 대화 [dae-hwa]
33	pronunciation	✔ 발음 [bal-ŭm]	벼름 [byŏ-rŭm]	바람 [ba-ram]	버릇 [bŏ-rŭt]
34	pencil	✔ 연필 [yŏn-pil]	연습 [yŏn-sŭp]	예복 [ye-bok]	예습 [ye-sŭp]
35	paper	장인 [jang-in]	✔ 종이 [jong-i]	지연 [ji-yŏn]	종 [jong]
36	tree	내용 [nae-yong]	녹말 [nok-mal]	✔ 나무 [na-mu]	치과 [chi-gwa]
37	mountain	신 [shin]	✔ 산 [san]	상 [sang]	손 [son]
38	wind	보람 [bo-ram]	벼랑 [byŏ-rang]	바름 [ba-rŭm]	✔ 바람 [ba-ram]

No.	Word	Option	Option
39	mushroom	변신 [byŏn-shin]	✔ 버섯 [bŏ-sŏt]
		변심 [byŏn-shim]	부산 [bu-san]
40	needle	비누 [bi-nu]	비늘 [bi-nŭl]
		✔ 바늘 [ba-nŭl]	나비 [na-bi]
41	notebook	✔ 공책 [gong-chaek]	혜택 [hye-taek]
		책임 [chaek-im]	이해 [i-hae]
42	professor	교회 [gyo-hoe]	치수 [chi-su]
		기회 [gi-hoe]	✔ 교수 [gyo-su]
43	doll	✔ 인형 [in-hyŏng]	형제 [hyŏng-je]
		안경 [an-gyŏng]	풍경 [pung-gyŏng]
44	department store	✔ 백화점 [baek-hwa-jŏm]	무지개 [mu-ji-gae]
		배추 [bae-chu]	김장 [gim-jang]
45	crystal	소장 [so-jang]	✔ 수정 [su-jŏng]
		수장 [su-jang]	소정 [sŏ-jung]
46	question	시험 [shi-hŏm]	향수 [hyang-su]
		✔ 질문 [jil-mun]	해답 [hae-dap]
47	cell phone	자전거 [ja-jŏn-gŏ]	✔ 휴대폰 [hyu-dae-pon]
		침대 [chim-dae]	지갑 [ji-gap]
48	post office	백화점 [baek-hwa-jŏm]	경찰서 [gyŏng-chal-sŏ]
		상점 [sang-jŏm]	✔ 우체국 [u-che-guk]

No.	Word	Option	Option
49	homework	성과 [sŏng-gwa]	생가 [saeng-ga]
		✔ 숙제 [suk-je]	성인 [sŏng-in]
50	pants	배영 [bae-yŏng]	바람 [ba-ram]
		반사 [ban-sa]	✔ 바지 [ba-ji]
51	clock	시간 [shi-gan]	시차 [shi-cha]
		✔ 시계 [shi-gye]	시야 [shi-ya]
52	skirt	치과 [chi-gwa]	하마 [ha-ma]
		목도리 [mok-do-ri]	✔ 치마 [chi-ma]
53	toy	운동장 [un-dong-jang]	✔ 장난감 [jang-jan-gam]
		도구 [do-gu]	악기 [ak-gi]
54	chair	액자 [aek-ja]	패자 [pae-ja]
		✔ 의자 [ŭi-ja]	책상 [chaek-sang]
55	underwear	잠옷 [jam-ot]	겉옷 [gŏt-ot]
		옷장 [ot-jang]	✔ 속옷 [sok-ot]
56	handshake	박수 [bak-su]	세수 [se-su]
		치수 [chi-su]	✔ 악수 [ak-su]
57	rainbow	찌개 [chi-gae]	태풍 [tae-pung]
		✔ 무지개 [mu-ji-gae]	태양 [tae-yang]
58	shadow	기름 [gi-rŭm]	구름 [gu-rŭm]
		거름 [gŏ-rŭm]	✔ 그림자 [gŭ-rim-ja]

No.	Word	Option	Option
59	wrong answer	답신 [dap-shin]	✔ 오답 [o-dap]
		문답 [mun-dap]	정답 [jŏng-dap]
60	favor	부부 [bu-bu]	✔ 부탁 [bu-tak]
		반사 [ban-sa]	배신 [bae-shin]
61	electricity	종류 [jong-ryu]	✔ 전기 [jŏn-gi]
		장기 [jang-gi]	전사 [jŏn-sa]
62	waste	기러기 [gi-rŏ-gi]	그림 [gŭ-rim]
		✔ 쓰레기 [ssŭ-re-gi]	가르기 [ga-rŭ-gi]
63	dictionary	수전 [su-jŏn]	시전 [shi-jŏn]
		생전 [saeng-jŏn]	✔ 사전 [sa-jŏn]
64	religion	✔ 종교 [jong-gyo]	정기 [jŏng-gi]
		장가 [jang-ga]	종기 [jong-gi]
65	envelope	✔ 봉투 [bong-tu]	방지 [bang-ji]
		봉지 [bong-ji]	빙자 [bing-ja]
66	salt	양념 [yang-nyŏm]	✔ 소금 [so-gŭm]
		반찬 [ban-chan]	휴지 [hyu-ji]
67	sugar	식초 [shik-cho]	후추 [hu-chu]
		✔ 설탕 [gŏn-gang]	배추 [bae-chu]
68	soy sauce	긴장 [gin-jang]	김장 [gim-jang]
		✔ 간장 [gan-jang]	건강 [gŏn-gang]

No.	Word	Option	Option
69	country/nation	✔ 나라 [na-ra]	누리 [nu-ri]
		노래 [no-rae]	내리 [nae-ri]
70	cleaning (a room)	채소 [chae-so]	✔ 청소 [chŏng-so]
		친구 [chin-gu]	칭송 [ching-song]
71	memory	✔ 기억 [gi-ŏk]	기록 [gi-rok]
		기념 [gi-nyŏm]	기밀 [gi-mil]
72	season	치과 [chi-gwa]	✔ 치과 [chi-gwa]
		치과 [chi-gwa]	치과 [chi-gwa]
73	machine	지게 [ji-ge]	비계 [bi-gye]
		✔ 기계 [gi-gye]	세계 [se-gye]
74	refrigerator	창문 [chang-mun]	부엌 [bu-ŏk]
		✔ 냉장고 [naeng-jang-go]	거실 [gŏ-shil]
75	correct answer	답신 [dap-shin]	✔ 정답 [jŏng-dap]
		답례 [dap-rye]	답보 [dap-bo]
76	car	마루 [ma-ru]	✔ 자동차 [ja-dong-cha]
		치과 [chi-gwa]	바퀴 [ba-kwi]
77	river	✔ 강 [gang]	가위 [ga-wi]
		개인 [gae-in]	길 [gil]
78	trip	이행 [i-haeng]	✔ 여행 [yŏ-haeng]
		야행 [ya-haeng]	요행 [yo-haeng]

79	number	수술 [su-sul]	기록 [gi-rok]	✔ 숫자 [sut-ja]	가루 [ga-ru]
80	dining table	식기 [shik-gi]	식료 [shik-ryo]	식사 [shik-sa]	✔ 식탁 [shik-tak]
81	button	당근 [dang-gŭm]	호박 [ho-bak]	✔ 단추 [dan-chu]	한밤 [han-bam]
82	money	솜 [som]	곰 [gom]	몸 [mom]	✔ 돈 [don]
83	glove	✔ 장갑 [chi-gwa]	선동 [sŏn-dong]	고무 [go-mu]	양복 [yang-bok]
84	shoe(s)	신장 [shin-jang]	✔ 신발 [shin-bal]	심장 [shim-jang]	가발 [ga-bal]
85	desk	책장 [chaek-jang]	체면 [che-myŏn]	책가방 [chaek-ga-bang]	✔ 책상 [chaek-sang]
86	screen	✔ 화면 [hwa-myŏn]	초면 [cho-myŏn]	가면 [ga-myŏn]	대면 [dae-myŏn]
87	advertisement	개인 [gae-in]	판광 [gwan-gwang]	✔ 광고 [gwang-go]	기강 [gi-gang]
88	breaking news	설명 [sŏl-myŏng]	전보 [jŏn-bo]	화질 [hwa-jil]	✔ 속보 [sok-bo]
89	recommendation	✔ 추천 [chu-chŏn]	초대 [cho-dae]	체조 [che-jo]	체육 [che-yuk]
90	mirror	가을 [ga-ŭl]	✔ 거울 [gŏ-ul]	기울기 [gi-ul-gi]	개울 [gae-ul]
91	rumor	소라 [so-ra]	소개 [so-gae]	소주 [so-ju]	✔ 소문 [so-mun]
92	airport	역 [yŏk]	✔ 공항 [gong-hang]	바닥 [ba-dak]	정류장 [jŏng-ryu-jang]
93	history	예의 [ye-ŭi]	병원 [byŏng-wŏn]	비밀 [bi-mil]	✔ 역사 [yŏk-sa]
94	future	지금 [ji-gŭm]	태도 [tae-do]	✔ 미래 [mi-rae]	미술 [mi-sul]
95	past	내일 [nae-il]	✔ 과거 [gwa-gŏ]	어제 [ŏ-je]	미래 [mi-rae]
96	expectation	기침 [gi-chim]	후회 [hu-hoe]	바로 [ba-ro]	✔ 기대 [gi-dae]
97	reality	예고 [ye-go]	✔ 현실 [hyŏn-sil]	배분 [bae-bun]	치맥 [chi-maek]
98	accolade/compliment	하나 [ha-na]	해방 [hae-bang]	✔ 칭찬 [ching-chan]	마무리 [ma-mu-ri]

www.ingramcontent.com/pod-product-compliance
Ingram Content Group UK Ltd.
Pitfield, Milton Keynes, MK11 3LW, UK
UKHW061828190726
13853UKWH00009B/2491

9 791188 195480